108課綱
贏戰統測

20分鐘 稱霸統測

英文 閱讀測驗

隨書附贈解析本

吳昱樺 編著

- 坊間唯一主打「素養導向」的統測閱讀測驗參考書
- 全書收錄 7 大閱讀解題技巧與精選 14 大閱測主題
- 訓練考生 20 分鐘完成統測閱讀測驗單元

東大圖書公司

國家圖書館出版品預行編目資料

20分鐘稱霸統測英文閱讀測驗／吳昱樺編著.——初
版四刷.——臺北市：東大，2024
　　　面；　公分.——（贏戰統測）

　ISBN 978-957-19-3173-9 （平裝）
　1.英語教學 2.讀本 3.中等教育

524.38　　　　　　　　　　　107023089

20 分鐘稱霸統測英文閱讀測驗

編 著 者｜吳昱樺
創 辦 人｜劉振強
發 行 人｜劉仲傑
出 版 者｜東大圖書股份有限公司 (成立於 1974 年)

三民網路書店
https://www.sanmin.com.tw

地　　　址｜臺北市復興北路 386 號　（復北門市）　(02)2500-6600
　　　　　　臺北市重慶南路一段 61 號 (重南門市)　(02)2361-7511
出版日期｜初版一刷 2019 年 1 月
　　　　　　初版四刷 2024 年 2 月
書籍編號｜E806610
I S B N｜978-957-19-3173-9

東大圖書公司

作者的話 ◀

　　很榮幸有這個機會應東大編輯部之邀，編寫本書「20 分鐘稱霸統測英文閱讀測驗」，希望讀者們可以不用再害怕閱讀測驗，配合本書循序漸進培養閱讀技巧、加強英語能力。

　　全書採 14 回單元編排，解題攻略篇剖析 7 大閱讀測驗命題類型及答題策略，讓讀者在閱讀本書的過程中，可以熟悉這些題型並迅速掌握解題技巧。實戰測驗篇精選 42 篇閱讀測驗，按照難易度分為初階、中階、高階，讀者可依自身程度規劃學習進度。文章取材多元豐富、貼近時事及生活，更結合統測及新課綱的重要議題。初階為統測最新的「圖表」題型，而中階和高階的文章均附有架構圖，讀者可更快速理解文章大意，學習事半功倍。

　　透過本書系統式的學習，讀者可以增進自身英語實力，在面對統測閱讀測驗的挑戰，輕輕鬆鬆獲取高分。

國立埔里高工　吳昱樺　老師

本書特色

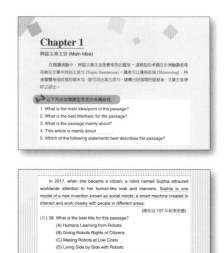

01

全方位解題攻略

7 大閱讀技巧編排，提升英文閱讀能力，輕鬆掌握文章脈絡。

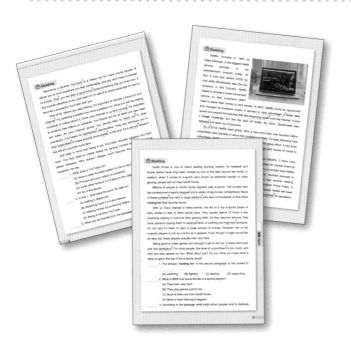

02

符合課綱議題的閱讀文章

精選 42 篇符合 108 新課綱議題文章，採程度分級設計，內容深入淺出。

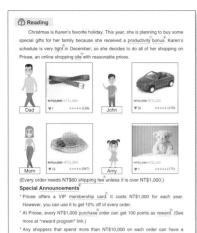

03

符合課綱理念「素養導向」
邏輯思考單元與圖表情境題一應俱全，迎戰
統測新題型。

04

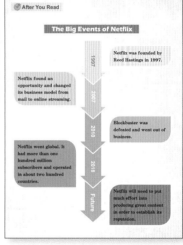

圖像式理念編排
圖像式設計，圖解單字與剖析文章架構，
學習效果事半功倍。

05

實用的練習題及中譯解析
每篇文章均附練習題，供讀
者檢視字彙及學習成效。另
附中譯解析本及詳盡解析，
讀者可以輕鬆自學。

目錄

解題攻略

閱讀測驗是各種英語能力測驗中的必考題型，主要測驗讀者對文章的理解程度，以及是否具備分析內文與推理上下文的能力。想要增進英文閱讀能力，除了平時大量閱讀，熟悉閱讀測驗題型，對於在測驗中獲得理想成績，也是不可或缺的。為此，在「解題攻略」中，透過七種常見命題類型並搭配統測共同科目英文歷屆閱讀測驗題目作說明，指導讀者如何在有限的考試時間內理解文章訊息，快速掌握解題重點。

閱讀測驗常見命題類型如下：

1. 辨認文章主旨 (Main Idea)

2. 作者撰文目的及語氣 (Purpose and Tone)

3. 支持主題的論述細節 (Supporting Details)

4. 由上下文推測字義 (Words in Context)

5. 推論 (Making Inferences)

6. 辨認文章內代名詞字義 (References)

7. 圖表 (Graphs and Charts)

Chapter 1

辨認文章主旨 (Main Idea)

在閱讀測驗中，辨認文章主旨是最常見的題型。這類型的考題在於測驗讀者是否能在文章中找到主題句 (Topic Sentence)。讀者可以運用略讀 (Skimming)，快速瀏覽每個段落的首末句，即可找出其主題句。透過上述方法建構出段落間的脈絡，文章主旨便呼之欲出。

此類題型常見命題敘述：

1. What is the main idea/point of the passage?
2. What is the best title/topic for the passage?
3. What is the passage mainly about?
4. This article is mainly about _____.
5. Which of the following statements best describes the passage?

例題①

In 2009, in a mission to record the damage caused by Typhoon Morakot, Chi found that the landslides brought about by this typhoon buried several mountain villages, and many areas were covered in flood waters. When Chi learned about the serious harm of land abuse, he decided to quit his government job to make films.

During the filming of *Beyond Beauty: Taiwan from Above*, Chi had difficulties **raising** funds. To meet the total costs of some NT$90 million, he used up all his savings and even asked for a bank loan. After the successful release of the documentary in around thirty countries, Chi planned to make a sequel. On June 10, 2017, unfortunately, when Chi was shooting the sequel, his helicopter crashed in the mountains. Many were saddened by the news of his death, but Chi will always be remembered for his contribution to promoting environmental awareness. (擷取自107年統測考題)

(A) 37. What is this passage mainly about?

    (A) Chi and his concern about the environment.

    (B) The success of Chi's documentary abroad.

    (C) What Chi went through to save typhoon victims.

    (D) The scenery recorded by Chi in his documentary.

答題說明

由第一段末句所描述，齊柏林了解到土地濫用的危害後，決定辭去政府的工作轉而投入拍片，以及第二段末提到他因推廣環保意識所做出的貢獻而被記得，可得知本篇文章主旨在述說齊柏林對環境的關注，故選 (A)。

例題②

    In 2017, when she became a citizen, a robot named Sophia attracted worldwide attention to her human-like look and manners. Sophia is one model of a new invention known as social robots, a smart machine created to interact and work closely with people in different areas.

(擷取自107年統測考題)

(D) 38. What is the best title for this passage?

    (A) Humans Learning from Robots

    (B) Giving Robots Rights of Citizens

    (C) Making Robots at Low Costs

    (D) Living Side by Side with Robots

答題說明

由本段末句可找到主題句，也就是社交機器人在現今已被廣泛運用在人類的生活中，故 (D) 選項是本文最適當的標題。

Chapter 2

作者撰文目的及語氣 (Purpose and Tone)

在閱讀測驗中，作者撰文目的可略分為兩種：告知或說服。文章作者對於該主題的態度會在用字遣詞和例證中明確表現出來。用以告知讀者資訊的文章，通常會以客觀的事例佐證；然而用來說服讀者的文章，作者則會針對主題，採用贊同或反對的觀點進行說明。

要找出作者撰文的目的和語氣，可從以下三個方向著手：

1. 找出文章中所列的例證。
2. 區別例證中，哪些為引述事實，而哪些是作者個人看法。
3. 例證中出現情緒的形容字詞，通常就是作者的語氣。

此類題型常見命題敘述：

1. What is the author's attitude toward _____?
2. What does the author think about _____?
3. According to the passage, what is the attitude/tone of the author?

例題

(i) Since many think that the more money they have the happier they will be, they will make all the effort to earn money. Some even steal or commit crimes to become rich. Of course, we know this is wrong. (ii) Many wealthy people have found that, in spite of having all the possessions, they are not really happy. Some wealthy people live alone in gorgeous mansions yet die lonely with no family or friends around them. They have spent their lives trying to be rich, but in fact they are poor. (iii) It is a pity that they do not know the true meaning of happiness, without getting and spending money.

(擷取自104年統測考題)

(B) 35. According to the second paragraph of the passage, what does the author think about money?

(A) The more money you have, the lonelier you will be.

(B) We all need money to live, but it has little to do with real happiness.

(C) Only those who have spent their life to become rich know the meaning of real happiness.

(D) Over the years, money has made rich people wish to live alone.

答題說明

題目要讀者找出作者對金錢的看法。(i)、(ii) 兩句屬引述事實的例證。先是提到一般普遍認為財富能帶來快樂，再提到有錢人不一定快樂來推翻這個普遍認知。(iii) 句中出現 it is a pity (很可惜) 這個情緒字眼，再次強調作者的觀點——有錢並不代表真正的快樂，故選 (B)。

Chapter 3

支持主題的論述細節 (Supporting Details)

在閱讀測驗中，這個題型出現的頻率最高。說到如何找出文章中支持主題的論述細節，就必須利用掃讀 (Scanning) 的技巧，也就是快速瀏覽題目並找到題目中的關鍵字，接著回到文章中交叉比對找相對應的例證。

掌握以下要點，有助於快速定位文章的論述細節：

1. 注意利用 **5W1H** 分析法 (Who, What, Where, When, Why 和 How) 找出文章中符合這些問題的敘述。

2. 注意例證處的關鍵標記字，如：First..., Second..., Third...; Some..., Others...; For example/For instance, such as, like 等。

3. 注意文意轉折處的關鍵標記字，如：but, yet, however, while, on the other hand 等。

4. 注意表達因果關係處的關鍵標記字，如：because, since, as, for 等。

此類題型常見命題敘述：

1. According to the passage, which of the following is (**NOT**) true?

2. Which of the following is (**NOT**) mentioned/included in the passage?

During the filming of *Beyond Beauty: Taiwan from Above*, Chi had difficulties **raising** funds. To meet the total costs of some NT$90 million, he used up all his savings and even asked for a bank loan. After the successful release of the documentary in around thirty countries, Chi planned to make a sequel. On June 10, 2017, unfortunately, when Chi was shooting the sequel, his helicopter crashed in the mountains. Many were saddened by the news of his death, but Chi will always be remembered for his contribution to promoting environmental awareness. (擷取自107年統測考題)

(A) 36. Which of the following is **NOT** true when Chi was making *Beyond Beauty: Taiwan from Above*?

(A) Chi refused to accept funds from others.

(B) Chi tried to borrow money from banks.

(C) Chi had a hard time finding enough money.

(D) Chi spent all his money producing the film.

答題說明

從題目給的選項可推知要找的論述細節關鍵字是 money/funds。而回到文章中可以定位出本段都是和關鍵字有關的細節描述。第一句提到齊柏林在籌措資金上有困難,故 (C) 正確;第二句敘述齊柏林用光了所有的積蓄並向銀行貸款,故 (B) 與 (D) 亦正確。整篇文章並沒有提到齊柏林拒絕他人資助,因此答案選 (A)。

Experts say that traditional stores can keep their customers by selling goods that buyers may want to see and taste, or feel the material and try on before purchasing. The stores can also offer services to instantly set up or repair electronic products. In addition, stores can offer things that are difficult to ship, or provide goods to buyers more quickly than online stores. Experts say that traditional stores offer the unique social experiences and personal interactions that most people enjoy. A lot of emotions can occur in the final buying decision. Oftentimes, you need that last sense of "Wow, this is exactly what I want!" before you're ready to pay, and you can't always get that online.

(擷取自104年統測考題)

(A) 38. What is the advantage of traditional stores?

        (A) Buyers can feel the material and try on before purchasing.

        (B) Buyers receive shipments more quickly than online shopping.

        (C) Buyers can choose any time to get on the Web and shop.

        (D) Buyers can compare prices from different online vendors.

答題說明

由題目可知所有關於 traditional stores (傳統商店) 的細節敘述都可能是答案，因此細讀本段可發現在第一句提到，專家認為提供可體驗材質和試穿的商品，能夠讓傳統商店留住顧客，因此答案選 (A)。

Chapter 4

由上下文推測字義 (Words in Context)

這類的測驗題型主要測驗對單字片語的認識及用法的掌握程度。雖然英文單字片語無窮盡，但可從上下文的線索推敲出該字的字義。

這類型題目的命題方式大致分為兩種：1. 找出文章中符合某單字或片語的同義 / 近義字；2. 找出或推測某單字或片語在該文章中表示的特殊含義。

此類題型常見命題敘述：

1. Which of the following has the closest meaning to the word/phrase...in paragraph...?
2. What does the word/phrase...in paragraph...mean?
3. Which of the following can replace the word...in the first/second/third paragraph?

During the filming of *Beyond Beauty: Taiwan from Above*, Chi had difficulties **raising** funds. To meet the total costs of some NT$90 million, he used up all his savings and even asked for a bank loan. After the successful release of the documentary in around thirty countries, Chi planned to make a sequel. On June 10, 2017, unfortunately, when Chi was shooting the sequel, his helicopter crashed in the mountains. Many were saddened by the news of his death, but Chi will always be remembered for his contribution to promoting environmental awareness. (擷取自107年統測考題)

(A) 35. Which of the following has the closest meaning to the word "**raising**" in paragraph 3?

　　(A) collecting 　　(B) lifting 　　(C) moving 　　(D) promoting

答題說明

由畫底線的句子可以得知，齊柏林為了新臺幣九千萬的拍片成本，散盡積蓄甚至向銀行貸款，故可推知 raising 為「籌措、募款」之意，答案選 (A)。

People suffering from fever should also take in additional **fluids** to balance water loss. Pregnant or breast-feeding women need large amounts of water, too. Doctors advise mothers-to-be to drink ten cups of water daily and women who are breast-feeding 14 cups per day. All in all, water needs differ according to various factors and drinking proper amounts of water is key to good health. (擷取自105年統測考題)

(C) 39. Which of the following is an example of "**fluids**" shown in line 1 in the third paragraph?

　　(A) Milk candy. 　　　　　(B) Chicken breast.

　　(C) Orange juice. 　　　　(D) Hot dog.

Chapter 5

推論 (Making Inferences)

推論即為讀出文章的言外之意。面對此類型的題目，可從文章中所提供的訊息及例證，來做出合理的推論，即可找到答案。

此類題型常見命題敘述：

1. Which of the following can be inferred from the passage?
2. It can be inferred from the passage that _____.
3. What can we learn from the passage?

例題①

South Korea knows that K-pop is very important. In 2015, South Korea made $5 billion from selling K-pop music and related TV shows, films, games, and so on. Furthermore, because of K-pop, other Korean products like Samsung smartphones, Korean-made cars, and Korean-style clothes have become very popular.

(擷取自106年統測考題)

(C) 39. What can be inferred from the passage about other Korean products?

(A) They became cheaper and smaller.

(B) People got disinterested in them.

(C) People bought more of them.

(D) They were seen less often on TV.

從本段末句提到因為 K-Pop 造成的韓流，使得其他韓國出產的產品都變得熱門，可以推論出人們對韓國產品的採購量增加，故選 (C)。

例題②

Another way to use solar energy is to "trap" it. When sunlight passes through the glass windows and strikes the material inside, the solar energy changes to heat. This heat warms the air inside, so the air inside becomes warmer and warmer. This build-up of heat is called the greenhouse effect. Such kind of heating is called passive solar heating.　(擷取自105年統測考題)

(C) 34. Which of the following could be inferred from the reading passage?

　　　(A) There is only one way to use solar energy to produce heat.

　　　(B) People can enjoy using solar energy without worrying.

　　　(C) Glass can be used to change sunlight into a source of energy.

　　　(D) All places get enough sunlight to make solar energy.

從本段的第二句可以得知，當陽光穿過玻璃窗戶而照到室內的物質時，太陽能便轉換成熱。故可知選項 (C) 為正確答案。

Chapter 6

辨認文章內代名詞字義 (References)

　　這類題型只要對代名詞有概念，就不難作答。解題時，循著題目所問的代名詞處再往前看一兩行，就是答案所在的位置。但須特別注意的是，指涉詞不一定代表最接近的名詞，仍須由文意及單複數來判斷作答。

👆 此類題型常見命題敘述：

1. What does the word "**it**" in line...refer to?
2. The pronoun...in the first/second/third paragraph most likely refers to _____.

⬇ 例題①

Coal remains a critical component of the world's energy supply despite its image as a polluter. As an enemy of environmentalists, **it** creates so much pollution. In this case, coal still has the undeniable advantages of being widely available and easy to ship and burn. The biggest attraction is low cost, however.

(擷取自102年統測考題)

(C) 42. In line 2, what does the word "it" refer to?

       (A) Pollution.   (B) Enemy.   (C) Coal.   (D) Estimate.

答題說明

由畫底線的部分得知，煤雖然是能源供應的重要一環，但也造成許多汙染。it 指的是第一句的主詞──煤，故選 (C)。

⬇ 例題②

...We (Project Gutenberg team) love to hear about kids or grandparents taking each other to an Etext to *Peter Pan* when they come back from watching *HOOK* at the movies, or when they read *Alice in Wonderland* after seeing **it** on TV.

(擷取自101年統測考題)

(D) 48. What does the word **it** in line 11 refer to?

       (A) *Shakespeare*.   (B) *Moby Dick*.

       (C) *Paradise Lost*.   (D) *Alice in Wonderland*.

答題說明

it 代替的是前面提到的 *Alice in Wonderland*，故選 (D)。

Chapter 7

圖表 (Graphs and Charts)

　　圖表閱讀是國中會考的必考題型，107 年首次出現在統測試題。無關未來命題走向，圖表閱讀仍是日常生活中必備的技能。舉凡行事曆、時刻表、節目單、廣告傳單、長條圖、數據分析、天氣預報……等，都是常見的圖表題型。

　　圖表通常以精簡的方式呈現資訊，因此閱讀時並不會受到冗長句子的干擾。但須注意題目的訊息文字與圖表中的數據及圖例間的關連性。此類命題的方向通常為 1. 是否理解圖表中的關鍵字和數據；2. 是否能分析圖表中的差異；3. 是否理解圖表中最大及最小數值所代表的意義。

⬇ 例題

　　The following is the weather forecast for the next five days in Hualien. Answer the questions based on the given information.

Day	Mon.	Tue.	Wed.	Thu.	Fri.
Weather					
Chance of Rain	10%	0%	30%	80%	40%

(擷取自107年統測考題)

(C) 32. On which day is it most likely to rain?

　　　　(A) Monday　　　(B) Tuesday　　　(C) Thursday　　　(D) Friday

(A) 33. Jane is planning a two-day trip to Hualien. She likes sunny days, so which period would be the best choice for the trip?

　　　　(A) Monday to Tuesday　　　　　(B) Tuesday to Wednesday

　　　　(C) Wednesday to Thursday　　　(D) Thursday to Friday

答題說明

第 32 題：答題關鍵為在圖表中找出降雨機率最大的一天。由題目提供的圖片和數據相互對照下，即可發現週四降雨機率達 80%，為降雨機率最大的一天，故選 (C)。

第 33 題：答題關鍵為在圖表中找出連續兩日晴天的出遊日。由題目提供的圖表可找出是週一與週二，故選 (A)。

實戰測驗

實戰測驗篇共有十四個主題，包含各種知識性、生活化、歷史性等多元內容，符合各種英文閱讀需求。 本書將每一主題區分為 Basic Level (初階) 、 Intermediate Level (中階) 與 Advanced Level (高階) 三種程度的文章練習，幫助讀者循序漸進，累積英文閱讀能力。

書中的十四個主題包含：

1. 流行 Fashion
2. 人文 Humanities
3. 科技 Technology
4. 能源 Energy
5. 時事 News
6. 環境 Environment
7. 文化 Culture

8. 歷史 History
9. 運動 Sport
10. 醫療 Health Care
11. 旅遊 Travel
12. 藝術 Art
13. 職場 Career
14. 防災 Disaster Prevention

Fashion
Basic Level

⑦ Pre-reading Questions

1. Which online shopping site do you like to visit? Why do you like it?
2. What are the advantages of shopping online?
3. What do you usually shop for online?

🄰 Target Vocabulary

tight *adj.*
緊湊的

bonus *n.*
獎金

site *n.*
網站

purchase *n.*
購買

announcement *n.*
公告

🛍 Reading

Karen wants to buy some gifts for her family because she just received her productivity① bonus②. Since Karen's schedule is very tight③, she decides to shop on Pricee, a top-rated online shopping site④. These are what she wants to check out.

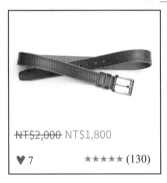

Dad

~~NT$2,000~~ NT$1,800
♥ 7 ★★★★★ (130)

John

~~NT$1,500~~ NT$1,200
♥ 20 ★★★★★ (150)

Mom

~~NT$2,300~~ NT$1,900
♥ 13 ★★★★★ (367)

Amy

~~NT$1,190~~ NT$1,150
♥ 7 ★★★★★ (175)

Orders & Shopping Information

* Free shipping is only available for order amount over NT$1,000. Otherwise, NT$60 shipping fee⑤ will be charged.
* Sign up your Pricee VIP membership card⑥! It costs only NT$1,000 every year. However, you can use it to get 10% off every order.
* At Pricee, every NT$1,000 purchase⑦ can get 100 points as reward⑧. (See more at "reward program" link.)
* We provide good after-sales service⑨. Return anything you buy within 7 days and get your money back. You only need to pay for return shipping fee.

Special Announcement⑩

* Any shoppers that spend more than NT$10,000 on each order can have a chance to enter the lucky draw for a round-trip air ticket to Tokyo.

_____ 1. Karen is a VIP at Pricee. How much does she have to pay for all the Christmas gifts?

(A) 6,050.   (B) 7,050.   (C) 5,445.   (D) 6,500.

_____ 2. If Mom is not satisfied with her hat, what can she do?

(A) She can enter the lucky draw to get another free hat.

(B) She can return the hat within 7 days and get money back.

(C) She can get a full refund of NT$2,300 if she returns the hat.

(D) She can send the hat back and get 100 reward points.

Ⓐ Word Bank

1. productivity [ˌprodʌk`tɪvətɪ] n. [U] 生產績效
2. bonus [`bonəs] n. [C] 獎金；紅利
3. tight [taɪt] adj. 緊湊的
4. site [saɪt] (= website) n. [C] 網站
5. shipping fee n. [C] 運費
6. membership card n. [C] 會員卡
7. purchase [`pɝtʃəs] n. [C][U] 購買
8. reward [rɪ`wɔrd] n. [C][U] 獎賞
9. after-sales service n. [U] 售後服務
10. announcement [ə`naʊnsmənt] n. [C] 公告；聲明

✎ Practice   請將 Word Bank 中的單字填入空格，並依句意做出適當變化

1. Nowadays, robots are widely used in the factory to increase _____.
2. The company offers a car as a _____ to motivate the employees to boost the sales.
3. Gina's boss was very generous; she gave her a big year-end _____.
4. When it comes to the Internet, people will surely think of social networking _____.
5. The teacher's wedding _____ surprised all of her students.

Fashion
Intermediate Level

⑦ Pre-reading Questions

1. What is an internet celebrity?

2. What makes people want to post videos about themselves?

3. How can people make money by being a YouTuber?

🔤 Target Vocabulary

earn a living *phr.*
賺錢謀生

channel *n.*
頻道

up and running *phr.*
運轉

partnership *n.*
夥伴關係

win-win *adj.*
雙贏的

📖 Reading

Becoming a full-time YouTuber① is a dream job for many young people. **It** allows you to work anywhere you feel comfortable, and you don't have to answer to a boss. Plus②, you can earn a good living③ doing something that you truly love. If this sounds attractive to you, just read on! I'm about to share some tips on how to become a successful YouTuber with you.

First of all, before you start filming, it's important to choose a focus for your channel④. Try selecting a subject you have a passion for, since you will be making hundreds of videos about it. Once your channel is up and running⑤, it's important to produce new videos on schedule. You should aim for at least one new video per week. As your channel grows, you should start to reach out⑥ to other successful YouTubers for partnership⑦ opportunities. They can introduce you to their subscribers⑧ to make yourself more visible⑨. In the end, it's a win-win⑩ situation that will win you both more fans.

Just keep in mind that being a top YouTuber requires patience and hard work. You may need to create videos for several months before you start to attract followers. Who knows? Maybe you'll become the next big Internet superstar one day.

_____ 1. In line 1, what does the word "**it**" refer to?

    (A) Getting a dream job.

    (B) Attracting more YouTube viewers.

    (C) Making money by producing videos.

    (D) Being a full-time YouTuber.

_____ 2. What makes a successful YouTuber?

    (A) Having a really focused subject for his or her channel.

    (B) Producing and posting videos on schedule.

    (C) Inviting other famous YouTubers in the video.

    (D) All of the above.

3. What can be inferred from the passage about YouTubers?

    (A) Becoming a YouTuber is the best job in the world.

    (B) What people like to watch should be YouTubers' concern.

    (C) Partnerships make it easier for YouTubers to become popular.

    (D) It takes several months for a YouTuber to make a video.

🎯 After You Read

How to Be a Successful Internet Celebrity

- ● Choose a subject you have a passion for before you start filming.

- ● Produce new videos regularly, at least one new video per week.

- ● Reach out for partnerships with other famous YouTubers to create a win-win situation.

- ● Patience and hard work are basic requirements to be a top YouTuber.

A Word Bank

1. YouTuber [`jutubɚ] *n.* [C] 在 YouTube 上傳原創影片的網路名人
2. plus [plʌs] *conj.* 並且；而且
3. earn a living *phr.* 賺錢謀生
4. channel [`tʃænḷ] *n.* [C] 頻道
5. up and running *phr.* (尤指系統或機器) 運轉

6. reach out *phr.* 和……交涉
7. partnership [`pɑrtnɚˌʃɪp] *n.* [U][C] 夥伴關係
8. subscriber [səb`skraɪbɚ] *n.* [C] 訂閱者
9. visible [`vɪzəbḷ] *adj.* 引人注目的
10. win-win *adj.* 雙贏的

Practice 請將 Word Bank 中的單字填入空格，並依句意做出適當變化

1. The show is on! I need the remote control to change _____.
2. This photography exhibition collaborated with some famous _____ to attract attention.
3. It only took this singer 5 years to become a highly _____ superstar.
4. Tim has been in _____ with Kyle, based on mutual trust and understanding.
5. It's a _____ situation. Both of us will achieve success through this project.

Unit 1

Fashion
Advanced Level

② Pre-reading Questions

1. How do you usually watch a movie? Do you go to the cinema, rent a DVD, or watch it online?

2. What are the online video services that you know? Which one do you prefer and why?

3. Do you like to watch videos online? What are the advantages and disadvantages of watching videos online?

🄰 Target Vocabulary

streaming media *n.*
串流媒體

defeat *vt.*
擊敗

budget *n.*
預算

restriction *n.*
限制

series *n.*
系列節目

📦 Reading

Netflix, founded in 1997 by Reed Hastings, is the biggest media service provider in the entertainment industry today. At first, it sold and rented DVDs by mail while Blockbuster was the top company in this industry. Netflix hoped to provide a more convenient service so that customers didn't

need to leave their homes to rent DVDs. In 2007, Netflix found an opportunity and changed its business model. It decided to take advantage of① the Internet and transformed itself into a streaming media② platform. It was a **tough** challenge, but the risk paid off finally. By 2010, Blockbuster was defeated③ and went out of business.

As of④ 2018, Netflix went global. Now, it has more than one hundred million subscribers and operates in about two hundred countries. To keep attracting new subscribers, Netflix constantly improves its services with great effort. It has even started creating original TV series⑤ like *Stranger Things* and *House of Cards* to bring members much enjoyment.

Although Netflix is dominating the streaming video industry, it does have several competitors. For example, Hulu is trying to increase its market share by offering a cheaper plan for users. However, its video library is smaller than Netflix and its budget⑥ plan forces users to watch commercials. Another example is YouTube. It also launched⑦ a streaming service, but it has several viewing restrictions⑧. The biggest threat to Netflix comes from Amazon Prime Video. It offers a similar service and continues to expand. To stay ahead, Netflix will need to put much effort into producing great content⑨ in order to establish⑩ its reputation. Otherwise, it might become the next Blockbuster.

_____ 1. What's the main idea of this passage?

    (A) How Netflix is different from Blockbuster.

    (B) Various online video service providers available nowadays.

    (C) How Netflix establishes itself and its future prospects.

    (D) Features and limitations of streaming videos.

_____ 2. The word "**tough**" in the first paragraph has the closest meaning to

    _____.

    (A) difficult   (B) stubborn   (C) tense   (D) formal

_____ 3. What did Netflix achieve in 2018?

    (A) It beat Blockbuster in sales figures.

    (B) It offered its members cheaper plans.

    (C) It had millions of members worldwide.

    (D) It forced its members to pay more.

_____ 4. Which of the following features does **NOT** make Netflix stand out from others?

    (A) It has its own original TV series.

    (B) It is the cheapest streaming service provider.

    (C) It has less viewing restrictions than YouTube does.

    (D) It is the pioneer in the streaming video industry.

_____ 5. According to the passage, which of the following statements is true?

    (A) Blockbuster and Netflix are owned by the same company.

    (B) Amazon Prime Video is probably the biggest competitor of Netflix.

    (C) TV series like _House of Cards_ is only available on YouTube.

    (D) Hulu offers cheaper plans with several viewing restrictions.

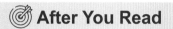 **After You Read**

The Big Events of Netflix

1997

Netflix was founded by Reed Hastings.

Netflix found an opportunity and changed its business model. Instead of selling and renting DVDs by mail, it turned into a streaming video provider.

2007

Netflix defeated Blockbuster and made it go out of business.

2010

Netflix went global. It had more than one hundred million subscribers and operated in about two hundred countries.

2018

Netflix will need to put much effort into producing great content in order to establish its reputation.

Future

Ⓐ Word Bank

1. take advantage of *phr.* 利用
2. streaming media *n.* [U] 串流媒體
3. defeat [dɪ`fit] *vt.* 擊敗
4. as of *phr.* 自……起
5. series [`sɪrɪz] *n.* [C] (電視或廣播的) 系列節目
6. budget [`bʌdʒɪt] *n.* [C] 預算
7. launch [lɔntʃ] *vt.* 推出
8. restriction [rɪ`strɪkʃən] *n.* [C] 限制
9. content [`kɑntɛnt] *n.* [U][C] 內容
10. establish [ə`stæblɪʃ] *vt.* 確立

✎ Practice   請將 Word Bank 中的單字填入空格，並依句意做出適當變化

1. To everyone's surprise, the young candidate _____ his opponent and won the election.
2. The president failed to fulfill his promise to increase the education _____.
3. Ann hadn't read the email and didn't know about its _____.
4. Jean's family has _____ close relations with her husband's family after their marriage.
5. Adam fell asleep and missed the final episode of his favorite TV _____.

 Answer Key   1. defeated 2. budget(s) 3. contents 4. established 5. series

Unit 2

Humanities
Basic Level

⑦ **Pre-reading Questions**

1. Who is your favorite author? What do you know about him/her?
2. What can you find in folded flaps (折口) of a book cover?

🔠 **Target Vocabulary**

leisure *n.*
空閒

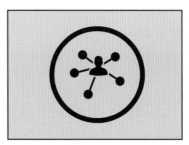

distributor *n.*
發行人

translator *n.*
譯者

fluent *adj.*
流利的

superb *adj.*
極好的

 Reading

Jacque Durand

Durand is one of the hottest young chefs in Europe. At an early age, he developed his interest in cooking. After graduating from Le Cordon Bleu, a well-known cooking school in Paris, he worked under Chef Emmanuel Olivier for two years. In Durand's leisure① time, he enjoys playing the guitar and watching soccer games on TV.

Taylor Smith

Over the past decade, Smith has been the main distributor② of Restaurant Review for *The New York Times*. Her colorful way of describing dishes has won her thousands of fans worldwide. Not just a food critic, Smith is also a language genius③. She speaks four languages including French, Chinese, German, and English.

Christine Lee

Lee is a highly regarded translator④. She is fluent⑤ in English, French, German, and her mother tongue⑥, Chinese. With her superb⑦ language talent, she has translated several classic novels into English. Most of her translated books are best-sellers⑧ on Amazon.

_____ 1. Which of the following is true about Jacque Durand?

    (A) He is a highly regarded translator.

    (B) He and Emmanuel Olivier used to be classmates.

    (C) He speaks French, Chinese, German, and English.

    (D) He is the author of *Street Food from Around the Globe*.

2. From the information of the book flap, it can be inferred that _____.

(A) music and sport are the inspiration for Durand's cooking

(B) *Street Food from Around the Globe* is a translation

(C) using colors to describe food is necessary for a food critic

(D) translators usually speak more than four languages

Ⓐ Word Bank

1. leisure [ˋliʒɚ] *n.* [U] 空閒;休閒

2. distributor [dɪˋstrɪbjətɚ] *n.* [C] 發行人

3. genius [ˋdʒinɪəs] *n.* [C] 天才

4. translator [trænsˋletɚ] *n.* [C] 譯者

5. fluent [ˋfluənt] *adj.* 流利的

6. mother tongue *n.* [C] 母語

7. superb [suˋpɝb] *adj.* 極好的

8. best-seller [ˋbɛst ˋsɛlɚ] *n.* [C] 暢銷書

✎ Practice 請將 Word Bank 中的單字填入空格,並依句意做出適當變化

1. As a famous film _____, Adam has made outstanding contributions to the movie industry.

2. Although Jim has lived in France for ten years, he still can't speak _____ French.

3. The food at the Michelin three-star restaurant is _____. It is not surprising that you have to make a reservation one year in advance.

4. More and more people nowadays have realized the importance of striking a balance between work and _____ activities.

5. With the assistance of a _____, the foreign visitor finally got to his destination.

⑦ Pre-reading Questions

1. How do you choose a restaurant when you want to eat out? Would the price or reviews play a part in your decision?
2. Have you ever watched any cooking shows? What is your favorite part of the show?

📖 Target Vocabulary

philosophy *n.*
哲學

invaluable *adj.*
寶貴的

artisan *n.*
工匠

purity *n.*
純淨

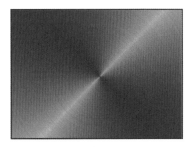

texture *n.*
質感

🏛 Reading

André Chiang is a Taiwanese star chef. In his career, the 42-year-old chef has won several awards for his unique cooking style, "Octo-philosophy①." Chiang believes that each meal should have *eight key elements to provide immense② satisfaction for his guests. He expects his dishes not only to be packed with flavors, but also to bring back pleasant memories.

Although Chiang was born in Taiwan, he spent most of his childhood in Japan. Initially③, he was expected to take over the family business, but he had much passion for food and wanted to become a chef. To fulfill his dream, Chiang moved to France, where he spent 15 years learning from the country's top chefs. These invaluable④ experiences inspired his imagination and stimulated⑤ his creativity. In 2010, he started his own restaurant, *André*, in Singapore, and he soon became a rising star.

In 2017, Chiang shocked the food world when he announced he was closing down *André*, his famous Michelin two-star restaurant. Chiang also gave back the Michelin stars he had earned. This decision allowed him to return to Taiwan and open his new restaurant, *RAW*. Now, his main focus is to train young chefs in Taiwan and to learn more about his native⑥ culture. "I'm happy and willing to be the window. That's my priority." Chiang said.

* Chiang's eight key elements are: salt, texture⑦, memory, purity⑧, terroir, south, artisan⑨, and uniqueness.

_____ 1. Why did André choose to close *André* in Singapore?

      (A) He was not making any money.

      (B) Michelin forced him to return the stars.

      (C) He wanted to shock the food world.

      (D) He decided to go back to Taiwan and achieve his ideals.

_____ 2. According to the passage, which of the following about André is **NOT** true?

      (A) He is training young chefs in Taiwan now.

(B) He learned his cooking skills in Singapore.

(C) He believes that "Octo-philosophy" can make his meals special.

(D) He grew up in Japan, but he was born in Taiwan.

_____ 3. In the last paragraph, what does André mean when he mentioned that he is willing to be the window?

(A) He wants to be a decoration like the window.

(B) He wants people to see him through.

(C) He wants his mind to be as clear as the window.

(D) He wants to share his experiences so that people can learn from them.

🎯 After You Read

② Although Chiang was expected to take over the family business, he had much passion for food.

③ Chiang spent 15 years in France, learning cooking skills from the country's top chefs.

① A 42-year-old Taiwanese chef spent most of his childhood in Japan.

André Chiang

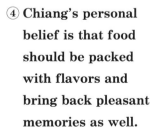

④ Chiang's personal belief is that food should be packed with flavors and bring back pleasant memories as well.

⑥ After Chiang closed his Michelin two-star restaurant in Singapore, he started his new life in Taiwan.

⑤ Chiang's unique cooking style, "Octo-philosophy", has won himself several awards.

A Word Bank

1. philosophy [fə`lɑsəfɪ] *n.* [U] 哲學
2. immense [ɪ`mɛns] *adj.* 巨大的
3. initially [ɪ`nɪʃəlɪ] *adv.* 最初
4. invaluable [ɪn`væljəbḷ] *adj.* 寶貴的
5. stimulate [`stɪmjə‚let] *vt.* 激發
6. native [`netɪv] *adj.* 出生地的
7. texture [`tɛkstʃɚ] *n.* [U] 質感
8. purity [`pjʊrətɪ] *n.* [U] 純淨
9. artisan [`ɑrtəzṇ] *n.* [C] 工匠

✏ Practice　請將 Word Bank 中的單字填入空格，並依句意做出適當變化

1. Ted's _____ of life is to seize the day and leave no regrets.

2. A white wedding dress symbolizes the _____ and innocence of the bride.

3. After years of practice, Vicky can speak French as fluently as a _____ speaker.

4. The experience of working overseas is definitely special and _____. It also makes your résumé impressive.

5. The _____ of the scarf was so soft that Emily decided to buy it.

ⓘ Pre-reading Questions

1. Do you like comic books? What makes comic books so appealing to you?

2. Who is your favorite comic-book character?

3. Who is your favorite comic-book writer? How much do you know about him/her?

🔠 Target Vocabulary

infectious *adj.*
有感染力的

dip *vt.*
浸

colleague *n.*
同事

editor *n.*
編輯

assign *vt.*
分配

🎩 Reading

In the world of comics, Stan Lee is a legend.① For over 75 years, he has served as a writer and an editor② of Marvel Comics. Throughout his career, he has created many well-known superheroes like Spider Man, Captain America, and X-Men.

The early years of Lee's life were filled with challenges. Lee was born in the early 1900s during the Great Depression,③ so he learned what it was like to struggle for survival. As Lee remembered, his parents were always trying to **make ends meet**. Not willing to deal with the reality, Lee often indulged himself in movies and books as a way to escape.

In 1939, with his uncle's help, Lee got a job at Timely Comics, which would later evolve④ into Marvel Comics. Initially, most daily routine assigned⑤ to him was fairly **humdrum**, such as dipping⑥ the pen in ink and ordering lunch for his colleagues.⑦ However, Lee had a chance to rise from rags to riches when the two top employees left the company in 1941. Lee took over their editing and writing responsibilities. Gradually, as his works accumulated, his name was introduced to the world.

One of the common characteristics of Lee's superheroes is that they are not perfect. For example, the incredible Hulk is extremely powerful, but he can't control his temper. Four of Daredevil's senses are stronger than normal people, but he can't see. What Stan Lee wants to express is making the unreal "real." The superheroes still have some weaknesses just like you and me.

In 2018, Stan Lee passed away at the age of ninety-five. Although Lee is no longer with us, his legacy and works are everlasting. Moreover, his enthusiasm toward comics is infectious,⑧ and it makes us fall in love with the characters he created.

1. According to the passage, we know that Stan Lee is a(n) _____.

   (A) writer   (B) actor   (C) painter   (D) superhero

2. The phrase "**make ends meet**" in the second paragraph means _____.

   (A) to meet one's end of life

   (B) to end the family relationship

   (C) to have enough money to get by

   (D) to make a circle by bringing two ends together

3. The word "**humdrum**" in the third paragraph is closest in meaning to _____.

   (A) boring   (B) melodious   (C) smooth   (D) challenging

4. What do the superhero characters that Stan Lee created have in common?

   (A) They are not perfect.   (B) They have bad temper.

   (C) They are blind.   (D) They are monsters.

5. What can be inferred from the passage?

   (A) Stan Lee enjoyed trivial chores like ordering lunch for people.

   (B) Stan Lee forced his colleagues to quit in 1941.

   (C) Stan Lee was not only a comic writer, but also a professional painter.

   (D) Stan Lee was inspired by the movies and books he knew when he was young.

After You Read

75 years dedicated to comic books

an editor, and Marvel comic writer

the creator of superhero characters: they are not perfect, just like you and me

Stan Lee

early struggle during the Great Depression— movies and books as a way to escape from the reality

famous works: Spider Man, Captain America, and X-Men

Ⓐ Word Bank

1. legend [`lɛdʒənd] *n.* [C] 傳奇人物
2. editor [`ɛdɪtɚ] *n.* [C] 編輯
3. the Great Depression *n.*
   經濟大蕭條
4. evolve [ɪ`vɑlv] *vi.* 逐步發展

5. assign [ə`saɪn] *vt.* 分配；指派
6. dip [dɪp] *vt.* 浸
7. colleague [`kɑlig] *n.* [C] 同事
8. infectious [ɪn`fɛkʃəs] *adj.*
   有感染力的

✏ Practice　請將 Word Bank 中的單字填入空格，並依句意做出適當變化

1. Over the years, the small shop has _____ into a large department store, and the number of its customers has increased dramatically.

2. As a professional basketball player, Michael Jordan is thought to be a _____.

3. Zoe is one of my _____. We have been working together for more than 20 years.

4. Before giving her baby a bath, the mother _____ her hand in the water to see how hot it was.

5. The government _____ the soldiers to assist the flood victims.

 Answer Key　1. evolved　2. legend　3. colleagues　4. dipped　5. assigned

Technology
Basic Level

⑦ Pre-reading Questions

1. Have you ever used Google Maps?

2. What are the features of Google Maps? How is it different from a traditional map?

3. How is GPS (global positioning system) used in our daily life?

4. Do you think Google Street View is a good idea, or a threat to privacy?

🔤 Target Vocabulary

riverside *n.*
河畔

buffet *n.*
自助餐

cocktail *n.*
雞尾酒

refill *n.*
續杯

fabulous *adj.*
極好的

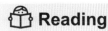 **Reading**

Dear friends,

To celebrate our graduation, I would like to have a party next Saturday. Come and have fun together! If you can make it, send me a LINE message by this weekend.

Time: September 22, 2018 3:00 p.m.～9:30 p.m.

Location: Number 6 Area, Dajia Riverside① Park

Phone number: 0912-321-321

Activities: special cocktails② (free refills③), fabulous④ buffet⑤ dinner, professional live band performance

Jeremy

Directions:

Take the MRT Brown Line toward Taipei Nangang Exhibition Center and get off at Dazhi Station. Leave the station at Exit 1. Then, take Bus 72 or Bus 222; get off at Dajia Elementary School Stop. Follow the signs for the Dajia Riverside Park. It might take you 7-10 minutes to walk there.

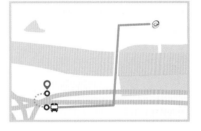

_____ 1. According to the invitation, which activity will **NOT** take place in the party?

(A) Fireworks.　　(B) Music.　　(C) Drinks.　　(D) Buffet dinner.

_____ 2. According to the directions, which is the suggested way to go to the party?

(A) 🚌 → Ⓜ → 🚶　　　　(B) 🚶 → 🚌 → Ⓜ

(C) Ⓜ → 🚌 → 🚶　　　　(D) 🚌 → 🚶 → Ⓜ

Ⓐ Word Bank

1. riverside [`rɪvɚ͵saɪd] *n.* 河畔
2. cocktail [`kɑk͵tel] *n.* [C] 雞尾酒
3. refill [`ri͵fɪl] *n.* [C] 續杯
4. fabulous [`fæbjələs] *adj.* 極好的
5. buffet [bə`fe] *n.* [C] 自助餐

✎ Practice 請將 Word Bank 中的單字填入空格，並依句意做出適當變化

1. Diana treated her colleagues to some _____ to celebrate her promotion.
2. On New Year's Eve, people flock to the _____ park to watch beautiful fireworks display.
3. The waitress asked the guest if he would like a _____.
4. There are various flavors of ice cream in the _____ lunch. Please help yourself to it.
5. The audience gave the _____ ballet dancer a round of applause.

Unit 3

Technology
Intermediate Level

⑦ Pre-reading Questions

1. What are the AI devices/services you have used? How do you like them?
2. What are the advantages and disadvantages that AI brings to our lives?

📖 Target Vocabulary

scan *vt.*
掃描

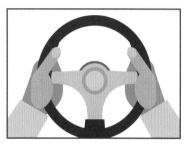

steering wheel *n.*
方向盤

artificial intelligence *n.*
人工智慧

analyze *vt.*
分析

harmful *adj.*
有害的

📖 Reading

Imagine a mobile① grocery store that comes to your front door. You simply enter the store, take the items you need, scan② them with your smartphone, and leave. Imagine going on a trip in an automatic③ car where you never touch the steering wheel④. Imagine children being taught in school by a robot. And imagine yourself checking into a hotel without having to stand in line. Can you imagine a life like this?

All of these incredible⑤ ideas are becoming a reality because of AI (artificial intelligence⑥). AI is a science that works to make computers think like humans. The origin of AI can be dated back to 1955, and it has gained so much importance because of the speed and the variety of data that can be collected and analyzed⑦. Although we may not have much knowledge of AI, our houses, cars, banks, and phones all use it. Its impact on our lives continues to grow. Moreover, AI has influenced almost every aspect of our lives, such as education, finance⑧, and even health care. We need to make sure it is used in ways that make our lives better, or it might be harmful⑨ to ourselves.

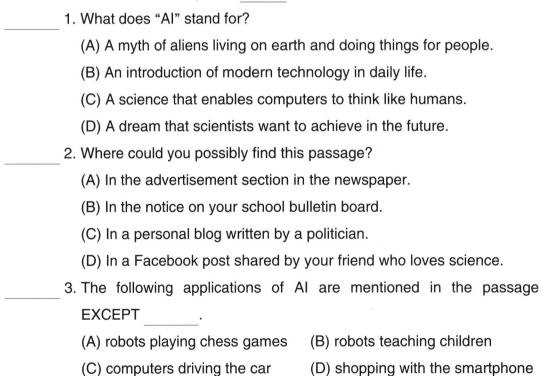

_____ 1. What does "AI" stand for?
   (A) A myth of aliens living on earth and doing things for people.
   (B) An introduction of modern technology in daily life.
   (C) A science that enables computers to think like humans.
   (D) A dream that scientists want to achieve in the future.

_____ 2. Where could you possibly find this passage?
   (A) In the advertisement section in the newspaper.
   (B) In the notice on your school bulletin board.
   (C) In a personal blog written by a politician.
   (D) In a Facebook post shared by your friend who loves science.

_____ 3. The following applications of AI are mentioned in the passage EXCEPT _____.
   (A) robots playing chess games   (B) robots teaching children
   (C) computers driving the car   (D) shopping with the smartphone

After You Read

Who are you?

I'm artificial intelligence, and you can also call me AI. I was born in 1955.

What can you do?

I can make computers think like humans.

Where can I find you?

I am everywhere. For example, in the stores, I help with the shopping. In cars, I help with the driving. In hotels, I help with the check-in. If you are interested, you can keep looking for me in your everyday life.

What's your relationship with human beings?

I was created to help human beings and make their lives more convenient. However, some people regard me as a threat because their position might be taken over.

A Word Bank

1. mobile [`mobḷ] *adj.* 可移動的
2. scan [skæn] *vt.* 掃描
3. automatic [ˌɔtə`mætɪk] *adj.* 自動的
4. steering wheel *n.* [C] 方向盤
5. incredible [ɪn`krɛdəbḷ] *adj.* 難以置信的

6. artificial intelligence *n.* [U] (亦可縮寫為 AI) 人工智慧
7. analyze [`ænḷˌaɪz] *vt.* 分析
8. finance [`faɪnæns] *n.* [U] 金融
9. harmful [`hɑrmfəl] *adj.* 有害的

✎ Practice 請將 Word Bank 中的單字填入空格，並依句意做出適當變化

1. To get the coupon, you just need to _____ this QR code here.
2. It is _____ that this five-year-old boy can play the violin so well.
3. After _____ the situation, we had a clear idea of what we should do next.
4. The world economic crisis will have a serious impact on our national _____.
5. The research indicates that smoking is _____ to people's health.

⑦ Pre-reading Questions

1. What is a drone? How are drones used in our lives?

2. Why are drones getting more and more popular/important?

3. Are there any disadvantages of using drones, despite their convenience?

🔠 Target Vocabulary

pilot *n.*
飛行員

fascination *n.*
入迷

warfare *n.*
戰爭

drone *n.*
無人駕駛飛機

handheld *adj.*
手提式的

🏛 Reading

Throughout history, people have been interested in flying and machines that fly. Today, this fascination① continues with drones② or, as they are formally known, unmanned aerial vehicles③ (UAVs). In short, a drone is a flying machine operated by remote control④, and there is no pilot⑤ sitting in it. Instead, a person on the ground with a handheld⑥ controller decides where the drone flies and what it does. Since drones are becoming more popular and being used for a wide variety of tasks, there has been much debate over their advantages and possible disadvantages.

On the positive side, drones have the potential to change the way many industries operate. For example, companies like Amazon will be able to use drones instead of trucks to deliver packages to customers. This can save both time and money. Also, the news industry can use drones to capture images in conflict areas, thus not only reducing risks but also protecting their reporters and camera operators. Finally, military applications of drones in modern warfare⑦ can carry out dangerous missions that would otherwise **endanger** the lives of pilots.

On the other hand, drones also raise some concerns. Safety and privacy seem to be two primary⑧ concerns when it comes to drones. For instance, since anyone can purchase and fly a drone, they could make the sky unsafe⑨. Besides, drones can collect any images without drawing attention, which makes people worry that drones may violate their privacy. For military reasons, some regulations⑩ on where and how drones can be flown are required. Drones should be prevented from entering a restricted⑪ zone, such as military bases and training camps.

Given the growth of the drone industry, we can't possibly resist or ignore drones in our lives just because of a few disadvantages. As long as we use drones properly, we can still enjoy the benefits they bring to our lives.

_____ 1. Which of the following is **NOT** a feature of a drone?

(A) There is no pilot sitting in it.

(B) It can be remotely controlled.

(C) There is no battery inside it.

(D) It is a flying machine.

_____ 2. Which of the following is **NOT** an advantage of a drone?

(A) To help in warfare.

(B) To deliver goods and packages.

(C) To reach a dangerous place.

(D) To invade people's privacy.

_____ 3. The word "**endanger**" can be replaced with _____.

(A) protect

(B) threaten

(C) limit

(D) embarrass

_____ 4. Why is it a problem when drones become easily accessible?

(A) They could make the sky unsafe.

(B) They will be more and more expensive.

(C) They might replace pilots.

(D) They will prevent many accidents.

_____ 5. What is the author's attitude toward drones?

(A) Concerned.

(B) Excited.

(C) Supportive.

(D) Indifferent.

After You Read

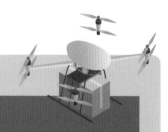

Drones (UAVs–Unmanned Aerial Vehicles)	
Advantages	**Disadvantages**
Drones can change the way many industries operate.	Drones can cause safety and privacy issues.
Supporting Ideas	
(1) Amazon uses drones to deliver packages to its customers.	(1) The sky becomes unsafe since everyone can easily own a drone.
(2) The news industry uses drones to capture images in dangerous zones.	(2) Personal and military privacy might be invaded.
(3) In the military, drones can carry out dangerous missions in warfare.	

Ⓐ Word Bank

1. fascination [ˌfæsn̩`eʃən] *n.* [U] 入迷
2. drone [dron] *n.* [C] 無人駕駛飛機
3. unmanned aerial vehicle *n.* [C] 無人飛行載具
4. remote control *n.* [U] 搖控
5. pilot [`paɪlət] *n.* [C] 飛行員
6. handheld [ˌhænd`hɛld] *adj.* 手提式的

7. warfare [`wɔrˌfɛr] *n.* [U] 戰爭；作戰
8. primary [`praɪˌmɛrɪ] *adj.* 主要的
9. unsafe [ʌn`sef] *adj.* 不安全的
10. regulation [ˌrɛgjə`leʃən] *n.* [C][U] 規則；法規
11. restricted [rɪ`strɪktɪd] *adj.* 限制出入的

🖉 Practice   請將 Word Bank 中的單字填入空格，並依句意做出適當變化

1. Tim has always liked to watch planes taking off and landing. Moreover, it is his dream to be a(n) _____ to fly a plane.
2. The water here is _____ to drink because it is heavily polluted.
3. The _____ source of income for the people here is tourism. Most residents make a living by selling things to the tourists.
4. This room is a(n) _____ area. Customers are not allowed to enter.
5. Attracted by Monet's paintings, Janet gazed at them in _____.

Energy
Basic Level

⑦ Pre-reading Questions

1. What information does the utility bill provide?
2. How much do you pay for the utility bill every month? Is it reasonable?
3. How can you pay the utility bill?

🗛 Target Vocabulary

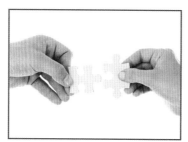

connection *n.*
連接

representative *n.*
代理人

rate *n.*
價格

invoice *n.*
費用清單

overdue *adj.*
過期的

Reading

Boston Gas and Electric Company

www.bostongasandelectric.com

162 Fenway Road, Boston, Massachusetts, USA

2020/03/05

This is to remind you that part of your balance with Boston Gas and Electric Company is past due①. Please make a payment immediately to avoid any interruption of your service. If we do not receive a payment within the next 30 days, we will be forced to cut off② your electricity. If that happens, you will need to pay your full balance and an extra $50 connection③ fee. If you are having any financial problems, please call us and we can help you come up with a payment plan. You can reach one of our representatives④ at 1-800-464-2729.

Account Number	Account Name	Service Address	Rate⑤
42729374937	Pauline Watson	342 Wilder Lane, Boston, Massachusetts, USA	Large General Service

Service Period		Invoice⑥ Issue Date	Bill Type	kWh Usage	Overdue⑦ Balance	Total Balance
2020/01/01	2020/01/31	2020/02/20	010	126,470	$160.81	$227.04

January 2020 Statement

Electricity Charge	$43
Gas Charge	$ 6
State Tax	$ 7.23
Late Fee	$10
Total:	$66.23

1. What is the purpose of this notice?

   (A) To notify the user of an unpaid bill.

   (B) To educate the user about how to read a bill.

   (C) To explain how the company charges for its service to the user.

   (D) To horrify the user since the company hasn't received the payment.

_____ 2. How much money will Pauline have to pay if she pays her bill in mid-April?

(A) $227.04.　　(B) $116.23.　　(C) $66.23.　　(D) $277.04.

Ⓐ Word Bank

1. past due *adj.* 逾期
2. cut off *phr.* 中斷
3. connection [kə`nɛkʃən] *n.* [U][C] 連接
4. representative [ˌrɛprɪ`zɛntətɪv] *n.* [C] 代理人
5. rate [ret] *n.* [C] 價格
6. invoice [`ɪnvɔɪs] *n.* [C] 費用清單
7. overdue [`ovɚ`dju] *adj.* 過期的

✏ Practice　請將 Word Bank 中的單字填入空格，並依句意做出適當變化

1. The principal met with a few student _____ to discuss a ban on bringing comic books to school.
2. Many people believe there is a direct _____ between a product's price and its quality.
3. The books will be _____ if I don't return them to the library today.
4. Most amusement parks offer kids special _____.
5. Please make a prompt payment once you receive the _____ of the course.

5. invoice

Answer Key 1. representatives　2. connection　3. overdue/past due　4. rates

Energy
Intermediate Level

⑦ Pre-reading Questions

1. How much do you know about Daylight Saving Time?

2. Why do we need Daylight Saving Time?

3. Do you think Daylight Saving Time is a good idea? Why or why not?

Aa Target Vocabulary

daylight *n.*
日光

question *vt.*
懷疑

disorder *n.*
失調

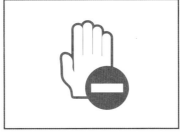

abolish *vt.*
廢除

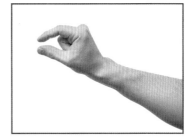

slight *adj.*
少量的

🛍 Reading

Every spring, people in around 70 countries "spring" their clocks one hour forward to begin "Daylight① Saving Time" (DST), also known as summer time. In the fall, they "fall" back one hour to standard time. George Hudson is credited with② proposing DST in 1895. It's a worldwide tradition, but its value is being questioned.③ For instance, because of its low efficiency and serious inconvenience,④ the Taiwanese government decided to abandon DST in 1980. Japan, South Korea, and China have cancelled this practice as well. Several states in the United States do not observe DST, and many others are in the process of abolishing⑤ it.

DST began in Germany in 1916 as a way to save energy and help people enjoy more light in the evening. However, some studies indicated that the amount of energy saved by DST was slight.⑥ It was also hoped that the extra hour of daylight would reduce traffic accidents and help boost the economy by encouraging people to go out at night and spend money. But neither of these happened.

Furthermore, many people have a hard time adjusting to time changes, especially those with sleep disorders.⑦ Being tired at work means less productivity. DST does not just affect humans, many farmers even notice a drop in egg production among their chickens during time changes. Today, the disadvantages of this century-old tradition may be greater than the advantages.

_____ 1. What is the best title for this passage?

(A) Daylight Saving Time Around the World

(B) The Origin and Practice of Daylight Saving Time

(C) Why Does Daylight Saving Time Matter?

(D) Is Daylight Saving Time Worth Saving?

_____ 2. The author's attitude toward DST is _____.

(A) positive   (B) negative   (C) mixed   (D) hard to tell

_____ 3. According to the passage, which of the following is true?

(A) George Hudson is a German who was born in 1895.

(B) DST is a perfect solution for people with sleep disorders.

(C) The value of DST is still being questioned.

(D) All Asian countries have stopped practicing DST since 1980.

🎯 After You Read

Introduction

Daylight Saving Time is a worldwide tradition. However, its value is being questioned since it is inconvenient and not effective.

Supporting Details

Inconvenience

- In the spring, people need to "spring" their clocks one hour forward and one hour backward in the fall.
- People with sleep disorders have difficulty adjusting to time changes.

Ineffectiveness

- The amount of energy saved is slight.
- The extra hour of daylight does not really reduce traffic accidents, nor does it encourage people to shop more to boost the economy.
- People and farm animals show low productivity.

Conclusion

The disadvantages of Daylight Saving Time are greater than its advantages.

Ⓐ Word Bank

1. daylight [ˋde͵laɪt] *n.* [U] 日光
2. credit sb with *phr.* 將……歸功於某人
3. question [ˋkwɛstʃən] *vt.* 懷疑
4. inconvenience [͵ɪnkənˋvinjəns] *n.* [U] 不便；麻煩
5. abolish [əˋbɑlɪʃ] *vt.* 廢除
6. slight [slaɪt] *adj.* 少量的
7. disorder [dɪsˋɔrdɚ] *n.* [C] 失調

✏ Practice 請將 Word Bank 中的單字填入空格，並依句意做出適當變化

1. Since Lisa's performance in the project was bad, her boss _____ her competence.
2. There has been fierce debate about whether the death penalty should be _____ in this country.
3. Amy's unexpected visit caused much trouble and _____ to my family.
4. There are only _____ differences between the twin brothers; it is difficult to tell them apart.
5. Due to too much pressure from work, Laura suffered from a mental _____. It took her three months to recover from it.

Unit 4

Energy
Advanced Level

ⓘ Pre-reading Questions

1. What is alternative energy?
2. What are some types of alternative energy that are being used?
3. What are the advantages of alternative energy?

🄰 Target Vocabulary

brake *n.*
剎車

renewable *adj.*
可再生的

windmill *n.*
風車

grid *n.*
輸電網

wind turbine *n.*
風力發電機

🛍 Reading

The Netherlands, a country which is famous for its charming windmills①, is now the world leader in wind power. One of the national railway companies, Nederlandse Spoorwegen, proudly claimed that all of its electric trains have been run on renewable② wind energy since January 2017.

How can trains run on the electricity generated by wind turbines③? Actually, these electric trains are specially designed. Unlike traditional trains, these unique electric trains don't have engines. Through the power grid④, the electricity is first transmitted⑤ from the high-voltage⑥ lines. Once the rail network receives the electricity, one of the ways to store the energy is to keep it in the batteries on board. The electricity also powers lights, air conditioners, brakes⑦, and computer systems in the train. Moreover, there is a circuit⑧ built in the train sending the unused electricity back to the power grid. This helps the railroad corporations⑨ reduce their electricity bills. According to the statistics, this system uses about 1.2 billion kWh of electricity a year. If we compare this amount of electricity with what is consumed in Amsterdam, which is said to be about 1.5 billion kWh of electricity year-round, we will find that wind power does have its potential.

You may wonder what the next step is after this breakthrough. Excited by the potential of wind power, the Netherlands is planning to build a vast⑩ wind farm on an artificial island in the North Sea. This new type of wind farm would **substitute** for the old ones and reduce the cost of energy by large-scale⑪ production. The wind farm will supply energy to the Netherlands, the UK and later to Denmark, Belgium, and Germany. In the near future, we may harvest the fruit of wind power not only in the transportation industries but also in other aspects of life.

_____ 1. What is the best title of this passage?

    (A) Electric Trains and Traditional Trains

    (B) Amazing Wind Power

    (C) The History of Nederlandse Spoorwegen

    (D) The European Union

_____ 2. It can be inferred from the passage that _____.

    (A) wind power is the best alternative energy

    (B) the wind farm in the Netherlands only supplies energy to the locals

    (C) the Netherlands plans to build the world's biggest wind farm

    (D) Nederlandse Spoorwegen is the only Dutch national railway company

_____ 3. Which of the following can replace the word "**substitute**" in the last paragraph?

    (A) Dominate.   (B) Shorten.   (C) Replace.   (D) Receive.

_____ 4. Choose the correct sequence of how electric trains are powered.

    (i) The electricity powers the train and other electric devices as well.

    (ii) The high-voltage lines send electricity to the power grid.

    (iii) The unused electricity goes back to the power gird.

    (iv) The rail power network sources the electricity and stores it.

    (A) i → ii → iii → iv   (B) iii → iv → i → ii

    (C) ii → iv → i → iii   (D) iv → i → ii → iii

_____ 5. According to the passage, which of the following is true?

    (A) The Netherlands is the only country in the world that has wind turbines.

    (B) Residents in Amsterdam consume electricity solely powered by wind.

    (C) The power on electric trains can't be stored in batteries.

    (D) The wind farm planned by the Netherlands will produce massive power for other countries.

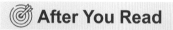
After You Read

Introduction	The Netherlands leads the world by using wind power. The wind-powered electric train is a significant example.
Body	How do electric trains operate on wind power? 1. The electric trains are specially designed and they don't have engines. 2. There are special devices such as batteries that are kept on board to save the energy transmitted from the power line. 3. The power is more than enough to make trains move. It is also used to supply other electricity needs in trains. 4. The unused power can be sent back to the power line and thus save cost on the electricity.
Conclusion	This innovation in the transportation industry shows a huge potential in wind power.

A Word Bank

1. windmill [ˋwɪndˏmɪl] *n.* [C] 風車
2. renewable [rɪˋnjuəbl̩] *adj.* 可再生的
3. wind turbine *n.* 風力發電機
4. grid [grɪd] *n.* [C] 輸電網
5. transmit [trænsˋmɪt] *vi.* 傳送
6. high-voltage [ˏhaɪˋvoltɪdʒ] *adj.* 高電壓的
7. brake [brek] *n.* [C] 剎車
8. circuit [ˋsɝkɪt] *n.* [C] 線路
9. corporation [ˏkɔrpəˋreʃən] *n.* [C] 集團公司
10. vast [væst] *adj.* 廣大的
11. large-scale [ˋlɑrdʒˋskel] *adj.* 大規模的

✏ Practice 請將 Word Bank 中的單字填入空格，並依句意做出適當變化

1. Andy's business proposal worked, and it has brought a(n) _____ amount of profits to the company.

2. It is important for a(n) _____ to innovate its products because it's the only way to survive in this challenging world.

3. The baseball game will be _____ live via satellite so that we can watch it on television.

4. The driver put his foot on the _____ pedal, and the car stopped suddenly.

5. Nowadays, scientists are eager to develop _____ energy to meet the increasing energy demand.

⑦ Pre-reading Questions

1. What is a claw crane? What are the prizes you can often see in it?
2. What do you think about the phenomenon of claw cranes sprouting up across Taiwan?

🄰 Target Vocabulary

rake in *phr.*
賺大錢

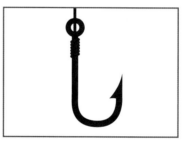

hook *n.*
鉤子

thrill *n.*
興奮

profit *n.*
利潤

skyrocket *vi.*
暴漲

The Daily News

Claw game stores have begun popular in Taiwan.

Today, there are more than 6,000 claw game stores in Taiwan. Have you ever wondered why the number of claw cranes① has skyrocketed② recently?

It seems that people like crane games because they are fun to play. If a person is lucky, he or she can win a cool prize with just NT$10. Nevertheless, this doesn't happen all the time. Players will usually spend more trying to win, and they often end up with nothing. Still, the thrill③ of playing keeps them coming back for more. For owners, crane game is a good business opportunity④. It costs only about NT$5,000 a month to rent a claw crane. Owners will earn money when someone plays the game and loses. The only thing owners need to do in this "lazy person's business" is to add new prizes and adjust the difficulty of the games. Some of the top claw cranes in Taiwan can rake in⑤ profits⑥ up to NT$150,000 per month.

No one knows how long crane games will remain popular. For now, it seems that **they** still have their hooks⑦ on people's wallets.

Unit 5 時事 News

63

_____ 1. The best title for this passage can be "_____."

    (A) Claw cranes Worldwide

    (B) How to Play Crane Games

    (C) Craze for Crane Games in Taiwan

    (D) The Price of Claw cranes

_____ 2. What does the word "**they**" in the last line refer to?

    (A) Crane games.   (B) People's wallets.

    (C) Lazy people.   (D) Crane game players.

Ⓐ Word Bank

1. claw crane *n.* [C] 夾娃娃機
2. skyrocket [`skaɪ͵rɑkɪt] *vi.* 暴漲
3. thrill [θrɪl] *n.* [C] 興奮
4. opportunity [͵ɑpɚ`tjunətɪ] *n.* [C] 機會

5. rake in *phr.* 賺大錢
6. profit [`prɑfɪt] *n.* [C] 利潤
7. hook [hʊk] *n.* [C] 鉤子

✏ Practice 請將 Word Bank 中的單字填入空格，並依句意做出適當變化

1. I hung the picture on my bedroom wall with a _____.
2. The price of property in this area has _____ ever since the nearby MRT station opened for operation.
3. Jaines had a great _____ to get a good job, but he gave up because he didn't want to work overseas.
4. Mr. Johnson manages his computer company very well and makes a lot of _____.
5. Watching the circus show is a big _____ for the children.

Unit 5

News
Intermediate Level

? Pre-reading Questions

1. What is a bandwagon? How is it related to the term "bandwagon effect"?
2. Can you think of some examples of people jumping on the bandwagon?

Aa Target Vocabulary

consumer *n.*
消費者

telecom *n.*
電訊

majority *n.*
大多數

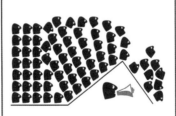

bandwagon effect *n.*
從眾效應

panic *n.*
恐慌

🛎 Reading

A telecom① service provider recently launched an unlimited② 4G internet deal at the price of NT$499 per month. Suddenly, mobile communication stores were packed with consumers③ eager to sign up for this special plan. Another wave of panic④ took place in grocery stores due to the speculation⑤ about the price hike in toilet paper. People flocked into the stores just to stock up⑥ on toilet paper. Do these stories sound familiar to you? Did you take part in them?

Actually, these phenomena⑦ are examples of the "bandwagon effect.⑧" It is a term in psychology which describes the behavior of people who follow what other people are doing. In 2008, Matthew Salganik and Duncan Watts, who are from Princeton University, carried out an experiment. They tricked the participants into believing a song was more popular than it actually was. As a result, the belief that most people consider the song a hit urged the participants to download and pay for the song without consideration.

Examples of people jumping on the bandwagon are ubiquitous.⑨ If you don't pay enough attention, you would easily be influenced by the majority,⑩ from where you eat, what you watch to even what type of job you should have. Once the bandwagon starts to roll, it is hard to stop! However, the majority's decision is not always right. We really need to think about what is the best before following the crowd.

_____ 1. According to the first paragraph, what is the purpose of describing consumers' wild behaviors?

    (A) To show how irrational people can be.

    (B) To prove that the deal is worth its value.

    (C) To teach the readers how to pick up a bargain.

    (D) To provide examples of the "bandwagon effect."

_____ 2. The "bandwagon effect" is a term used in _____.

    (A) agriculture   (B) architecture (C) education   (D) psychology

_____ 3. What does the author suggest the readers do before they make any decision?

(A) Never believe anyone because they may play a trick on you.

(B) Follow the crowd because the majority is always right.

(C) Think twice before taking any action.

(D) Jump on the bandwagon to avoid others' influence.

🎯 After You Read

Introduction
Have you ever jumped on the bandwagon recently?

1. People packed in mobile communication stores to get the unlimited 4G internet deal.
2. People flocked into grocery stores to stock up on boxes of toilet paper.

Body
What is the "bandwagon effect"?

The "bandwagon effect" is a term describing the behavior of people who follow what other people are doing because it is popular.

Conclusion
How do you stop yourself from jumping on the bandwagon?

The bandwagon effect is everywhere. It is hard to stay away from it.
You really need to think about how to make the best decision for yourself.

A Word Bank

1. telecom [`tɛlə,kəm] *n.* [U] 電信
2. unlimited [ʌn`lɪmɪtɪd] *adj.* 不受限制的
3. consumer [kən`sumɚ] *n.* [C] 消費者
4. panic [`pænɪk] *n.* [U][C] 恐慌
5. speculation [,spɛkjə`leʃən] *n.* [C][U] 猜測
6. stock up *phr.* 囤積；儲備
7. phenomenon [fə`namə,nan] *n.* [C] 現象
8. bandwagon effect *n.* [C] 從眾效應
9. ubiquitous [ju`bɪkwə,təs] *adj.* 普遍存在的
10. majority [mə`dʒɔrətɪ] *n.* [S] 大多數

✐ Practice　請將 Word Bank 中的單字填入空格，並依句意做出適當變化

1. The _____ of the audience voted for Kate and made her the champion in the beauty contest.
2. There are widespread _____ concerning the famous singer's death.
3. The rich man has _____ wealth. He never worries about money.
4. Nowadays, having one or more smartphones becomes a common _____.
5. The anniversary sale motivated _____ to make large purchases in the department store.

Answer Key　1. majority　2. speculations　3. unlimited　4. phenomenon　5. consumers

68

Unit 5

News
Advanced Level

❓ **Pre-reading Questions**

1. Do the elders in your family have any particular expectations for boys and girls?

2. How are kids raised in your family? Will one be treated differently because he/she is a boy/girl?

3. How do you like your gender role in your family?

Target Vocabulary

supportive *adj.*
支持的

equality *n.*
平等

democracy *n.*
民主

make-up *n.*
化妝品

liberty *n.*
自由

🎒 Reading

With many campaigners arguing that men and women should be treated equally, the issue of gender equality① has received a lot of attention in recent years. Taiwan, a country known for its democracy② and liberty③, has taken huge steps forward, and **it** proudly claims to have many female leaders and even a female president. With so much progress being made, lots of people have suggested that Taiwan no longer suffers from gender inequality problems. Do you agree with that? Well, looking at some statistics might help you understand the situation better.

According to the Directorate General of Budget, Accounting and Statistics (DGBAS), Taiwan ranked 38th in the world in terms of gender equality in 2016. In politics, only 38% of the country's legislators④ were women. In business, just 6% of Taiwanese CEOs⑤ were women. As for the education community, only 25% of high school principals and 7% of college principals were women. All these show that women in Taiwan still struggle to be seen in public.

Furthermore, life is also not easy for girls and women in Taiwan. Girls tend to be taught that they should be caring, gentle, and supportive⑥. At family gatherings, you will find that women do all the housework while men just sit down and relax. In the workplace, women are often required to put on make-up⑦ and uncomfortable business suits.

Although Taiwan still has a long way to go to be a gender-equal society, it is not alone. As a member of CALD (Council⑧ of Asian Liberals and Democrats), Taiwan has received a lot of support from other member countries and has been empowered⑨ along the way. For example, Taiwan has passed laws to create a gender-friendly environment for career women. That is, companies with over 100 employees have to provide childcare and nursing facilities⑩. Therefore, Taiwan really has made great strides⑪ toward gender equality, and we should be proud of it.

1. What is the best title for this passage?

(A) Women Suffering in Taiwan

(B) Gender Equality in Taiwan

(C) Gender Stereotypes in Taiwan

(D) Female Leaders in Taiwan

2. The purpose of presenting the percentage of female leaders in Taiwan is to _____.

(A) prove that Taiwan is making progress on gender equality

(B) show that Taiwan is not a gender-equal society

(C) demonstrate that Taiwan has a gender discrimination problem

(D) argue that women are doing better than men in the workplace

3. What does "**it**" in the first paragraph refer to?

(A) Democracy.

(B) Taiwan.

(C) Liberty.

(D) Gender equality.

4. Which of the following is **NOT** what girls/women are expected to do in Taiwan?

(A) Taking care of the baby.

(B) To be gentle and supportive.

(C) Being relaxed at family gatherings.

(D) Putting on make-up and suits for work.

5. We can infer that the author feels _____ about the gender equality situation in future Taiwan.

(A) positive

(B) concerned

(C) embarrassed

(D) indifferent

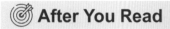

The issue of gender equality has received a lot of attention in recent years. Taiwan, a country known for its democracy and liberty, still has room for improvement in this area.

A reality check of gender equality in Taiwan	Gender stereotypes in life and the workplace

1. the 38th gender-equal country in the world in 2016
2. Female employment rate
  * In politics: 38% (legislators)
  * In business: 6% (CEOs)
  * In education: 25% (high school principals); 7% (college principals)
	1. Women are expected to be caring, gentle, and supportive.
	2. Women still do more chores at home than men.
	3. Women are required to put on make-up and business suits.

Career women in Taiwan have received a lot of support. The government is trying to create a gender-friendly environment for career women. Taiwan really has made great strides toward gender equality, and we should be proud of it.

A Word Bank

1. equality [ɪˋkwɑlətɪ] *n.* [U][C] 平等
2. democracy [dəˋmɑkrəsɪ] *n.* [U] 民主
3. liberty [ˋlɪbɚtɪ] *n.* [U] 自由
4. legislator [ˋlɛdʒɪs,letɚ] *n.* [C] 立法委員；立法者
5. CEO (= chief executive officer) *abbr.* 執行長
6. supportive [səˋpɔrtɪv] *adj.* 支持的
7. make-up [ˋmek,ʌp] *n.* [C] 化妝品
8. council [ˋkaʊnsl̩] *n.* [C] 委員會
9. empower [ɪmˋpaʊɚ] *vt.* 授權
10. facilities [fəˋsɪlə,tɪz] *n.* [plural] 設施
11. stride [straɪd] *n.* [C] 進展；進步

✎ Practice　請將 Word Bank 中的單字填入空格，並依句意做出適當變化

1. The idea of _____ is important when you are a parent. Your children want you to treat them equally.

2. In our university, students can use all sorts of educational _____, such as labs, lecture halls, and seminar rooms.

3. The people in the country fight for their _____. They want to be independent.

4. The core of _____ is that the government is chosen by the people through voting.

5. Although Ray lost the election to be a(n) _____, his followers wanted him to run for president.

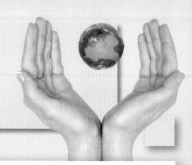

Unit 6

Environment
Basic Level

⟨?⟩ Pre-reading Questions

1. What volunteer work have you done in the past?
2. When you serve as a volunteer, what are the things you can get involved in?
3. How can you prepare yourself to be a volunteer?

[Aa] Target Vocabulary

coastal *adj.*
海岸的

sponsor *vt.*
贊助

efficiency *n.*
效率

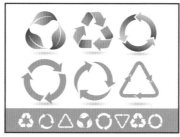

reusable *adj.*
可重複使用的

alliance *n.*
聯盟

 **Reading**

Let's Clean the Beach

Organizer[①]: Westfield Beach Association
Co-organizer: Ocean Cleanup Alliance[②]
Sponsor: Charlie's Bagel Café

You should wear and prepare
hat
scarf
T-shirt
sneakers

We will provide
pen
sack
backpack
bottle

The Westfield Beach Association (WBA) is holding a coastal[③] cleanup event on June 8. We're hoping to make it the biggest cleanup ever, so bring a couple of friends or family members—young or old!

This year, Charlie's Bagel[④] Café is sponsoring[⑤] this coastal cleanup and will provide every participant with coffee and bagels to keep them going and increase working efficiency[⑥]. Don't forget to bring your own reusable[⑦] cups and plates.

We will also hold a cleanup contest. Teams of four will compete to see which one can collect the most trash. The winner will get a mystery prize! See you soon!

_____ 1. Why did the Westfield Beach Association release this leaflet?

   (A) To encourage people to attend an event.

   (B) To emphasize the importance of family.

   (C) To ask companies to sponsor an event.

   (D) To raise public awareness of environmental protection.

_____ 2. According to the leaflet, which of the following items do volunteers **NOT** need to bring with them?

(A)   (B)   (C)   (D)

Ⓐ Word Bank

1. organizer [`ɔrgən͵aɪzɚ] n. [C] 籌辦者

2. alliance [ə`laɪəns] n. [C] 聯盟

3. coastal [`kostl̩] adj. 海岸的

4. bagel [`begl̩] n. [C] 貝果

5. sponsor [`spɑnsɚ] vt. 贊助

6. efficiency [ɪ`fɪʃənsɪ] n. [U] 效率

7. reusable [͵rɪ`juzəbl̩] adj. 可重複使用的

✎ Practice   請將 Word Bank 中的單字填入空格，並依句意做出適當變化

1. The four major airlines have formed a(n) _____ to provide better service.

2. The rich man donated a tremendous amount of money to the hospital, _____ its cancer research.

3. Simon always works with great _____; he makes good use of time to produce good results at work.

4. Instead of using disposable chopsticks, Anita always brings her _____ ones when eating out.

5. Keith has been a five-time _____ of this marathon. He knows every detail of the race.

Unit 6

Environment
Intermediate Level

? Pre-reading Questions

1. What do you think of climate change? How does climate change affect our lives?
2. How can you stop climate change from getting worse?
3. How can people combine technology with environmental awareness?

Aa Target Vocabulary

satellite *n.*
人造衛星

sculpt *vi.*
雕塑

dune *n.*
沙丘

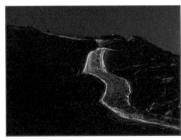

magma *n.*
岩漿

fingertip *n.*
指尖

🏮 Reading

Human activities are pushing Mother Nature to the limit, impacting the environment, changing the climate, and posing a threat to biodiversity①. Melting glaciers, shrinking jungles, and expanding deserts are Mother Nature's fightback. These phenomena heighten② our awareness of environmental protection, but how can young people learn about the environmental issues and take actions to stop them from getting worse? Some new games and apps③ use puzzles, quizzes, and virtual scenarios④ to educate the younger generation about this matter and show them how to help the earth.

An app called *Earth Primer* is like a science book for playful people. The player can discover how the earth works at the beginning of the game by creating mountains and growing forests. Then he or she can create some forces of nature with his or her fingertips⑤. The player can make volcanoes⑥, sculpt⑦ mountains, form glaciers, shape sand dunes⑧, push around tectonic⑨ plates, paint with wind, heat up magma⑩—and more! In addition, the game displays real-time satellite⑪ images. In this way, when natural disasters take place, the app can show how they work and allow the player to interact with the images. By realizing the changes that are truly happening on the earth, the app inspires the player to care about the earth more.

If young people do not learn about nature, they will not appreciate and protect it. More and more games or apps are invented to advocate⑫ for environmental protection in the hope that the earth will be green again one day.

_____ 1. What is the main idea of this passage?

    (A) Using games and apps can also help the environment.

    (B) Nothing can be done for the damaged earth.

    (C) *Earth Primer* is a perfect solution to environmental problems.

    (D) *Earth Primer* is a fun game for many scientists.

_____ 2. How can people help the environment by playing the green game?

    (A) They can make a credit card donation.

    (B) They can be aware of environmental issues through the game.

(C) The game will actually clean or change the environment.

(D) The game will help them start an environmental campaign.

_____ 3. Which of the following about the green game mentioned in the passage is true?

(A) It is free of charge and easy to play.

(B) It causes climate change and deforestation.

(C) It inspires young people to care about the environment.

(D) It monitors all kinds of pollution on the earth.

🎯 After You Read

It's interactive. Players can form some forces of nature and observe how they work.

It also shows how nature disasters are caused.

It's a game app showing how the earth was formed.

What is *Earth Primer*?

Hopefully, through this game app, players would be inspired to protect the earth.

A Word Bank

1. biodiversity [ˌbaɪodaɪˈvɝsɪtɪ] *n.* [U] 生物多樣性
2. heighten [ˈhaɪtn̩] *vt.*; *vi.* 使增強
3. app [æp] *n.* [C] 應用程式
4. scenario [sɪˈnɛrɪˌo] *n.* [C] 可能發生的事態
5. fingertip [ˈfɪŋɡɚˌtɪp] *n.* [C] 指尖
6. volcano [vɑlˈkeno] *n.* [C] 火山
7. sculpt [skʌlpt] *vt.*; *vi.* 雕塑
8. dune [djun] *n.* [C] 沙丘
9. tectonic [tɛkˈtɑnɪk] *adj.* 地殼構造的
10. magma [ˈmæɡmə] *n.* [U] 岩漿
11. satellite [ˈsætl̩ˌaɪt] *n.* [C] 人造衛星
12. advocate [ˈædvəˌket] *vt.* 支持；提倡

✒ Practice 請將 Word Bank 中的單字填入空格，並依句意做出適當變化

1. Alex was excited to participate in the program of launching a rocket with a communications _____ into space.
2. Felix _____ gender equality. It goes without saying that he opposes gender discrimination in the workplace.
3. The serious pollution poses a threat to _____ and makes many species die out.
4. The huge statue which the artist spent several years _____ is often referred to as his greatest masterpiece.
5. The functions of the smartphone, such as high-speed Internet connectivity and many interesting _____, attract many young people.

Answer Key 1. satellite 2. advocates 3. biodiversity 4. sculpting 5. apps

Unit 6

Environment
Advanced Level

? Pre-reading Questions

1. What are things you use in everyday life made out of plastic?

2. What can we do to make the best out of plastic?

3. Do you recycle? Why and how do you do it?

Aa Target Vocabulary

albatross *n.*
信天翁

fabric *n.*
織物

decompose *vi.*
腐爛

current *n.*
水流

straw *n.*
吸管

🎒 Reading

How many plastic products can we see? How many have we already thrown away? Where does plastic go when we are done using it? Virtually^① all the plastic ever produced—bags, computer keyboards^②, straws^③, and so much more—still exists. Unlike paper, fabric^④, and even metal, plastic

doesn't break down easily. It is said that plastic water bottles take 450 years to decompose^⑤ and thicker objects can take twice as long!

Plastic is nearly indestructible^⑥, and most of it ends up in the ocean. Once there, powerful ocean currents^⑦ bring it together into huge, swirling^⑧ patches of trash^⑨. The largest of these is known as the Great Pacific Garbage Patch. This garbage patch looks terrible, and it has an awful effect on marine^⑩ animals. For example, thousands of sea turtles drown every year after getting tangled^⑪ in plastic waste, and albatrosses^⑫ are affected in even greater numbers. These huge sea birds regularly eat small pieces of plastic, believing **it** to be food. Since albatrosses are unable to digest^⑬ the plastic, it stays in their stomachs, fooling them into believing they've eaten enough. As a result, hundreds of thousands of these majestic^⑭ creatures die every year.

We're responsible for these tragedies, and we have to do something about them. Recycling is important, but it's not enough. Since plastic lasts so long, the only solution is to stop using it. Stop using plastic bags, stop getting food wrapped^⑮ in multiple layers^⑯ of plastic, and stop buying throwaway plastic items when you can choose reusable alternatives. We've created this plastic nightmare^⑰, and only we can end it.

1. Why is plastic a big headache for the environment?

(A) It is difficult to decompose.

(B) It is very big and heavy.

(C) It is sea animals' favorite food.

(D) It is easy to break down.

2. What is the best way to end the plastic nightmare?

(A) Feeding albatrosses.

(B) Cleaning the ocean.

(C) Stopping using plastic products.

(D) Buying throwaway plastic items.

3. What does the word "**it**" in the second paragraph mean?

(A) The ocean.

(B) The garbage patch.

(C) Plastic waste.

(D) Sea animals.

4. According to the passage, which of the following is the victim of the plastic waste?

(A) Human beings.

(B) The ocean.

(C) Sea animals.

(D) All of the above.

5. What is the main purpose of this passage?

(A) To inform people how bad the environment is.

(B) To encourage people to use more plastic products.

(C) To stop causing all kinds of pollution.

(D) To raise people's awareness of conserving the environment.

🎯 After You Read

· Introduction

How many plastic products can we see? How many have we already thrown away?

Where does plastic go when we are done using it?

When is an end to the plastic cycle? It may take about 450 years for plastic to decompose.

· Body

Plastic is nearly indestructible, and most of it ends up in the ocean. A large number of marine creatures die every year because they swallow plastic or are trapped by it.

· Conclusion

We're responsible for these tragedies. To save our beautiful planet, we need to stop using plastic products and start using other alternatives. We've created this plastic nightmare, and only we can end it.

Ⓐ Word Bank

1. virtually [`vɝtʃʊəlɪ] *adv.* 幾乎；實際上
2. keyboard [`ki,bord] *n.* [C] 鍵盤
3. straw [strɔ] *n.* [C] 吸管
4. fabric [`fæbrɪk] *n.* [C][U] 織物
5. decompose [,dikəm`poz] *vi.* 分解；腐爛
6. indestructible [,ɪndɪ`strʌktəbl̩] *adj.* 難以銷毀的
7. current [`kɝrənt] *n.* [C] 水流
8. swirl [swɝl] *vi.* 旋轉
9. patch of trash *n.* [C] 垃圾帶
10. marine [mə`rin] *adj.* 海洋的
11. tangle [`tæŋgl̩] *vt.* 使捲入
12. albatross [`ælbə,trɔs] *n.* [C] 信天翁
13. digest [daɪ`dʒɛst] *vt.* 消化
14. majestic [mə`dʒɛstɪk] *adj.* 威嚴的；雄偉的
15. wrap [ræp] *vt.* 包；裹
16. layer [`leɚ] *n.* [C] 層
17. nightmare [`naɪt,mɛr] *n.* [C] 夢魘

✎ **Practice** 請將 Word Bank 中的單字填入空格，並依句意做出適當變化

1. Jenny sipped her orange juice with a(n) _____.
2. When you misspell a word, you can eliminate the error by pressing the "Delete" key on the _____.
3. Paris is a European city known for its _____ Eiffel Tower.
4. The clerk helped _____ the Christmas gifts for customers.
5. Last night, Paula had a(n) _____ about being chased by a monster.

 Answer Key 1. straw 2. keyboard 3. majestic 4. wrap 5. nightmare

Unit 6 環境 Environment

⑦ Pre-reading Questions

1. What's your favorite type of food?

2. Do you enjoy cooking or baking? If yes, do you have a foolproof recipe?

🄰 Target Vocabulary

chili *n.*
辣椒

serving *n.*
一份

garlic *n.*
大蒜

chop *vt.*
剁碎

spice up *phr.*
使……增添風味

 **Reading**

Here's a wonderful dish called "golden coin eggs" that will spice up① your meals. The recipe comes from Hunan, China, and it's easy to make.

Golden Coin Eggs

Cooking Time: 25 minutes
Servings②: 2-3 servings
Difficulty: Easy

Ingredients:

- 4 eggs
- 3 cloves④ of garlic⑤
- 1 tablespoon of flour
- Some chopped⑦ green onions and chilies⑧

- 1 inch of fresh ginger③
- 1/2 tablespoon of soy sauce
- 3 tablespoons of olive⑥ oil

Instructions:

1. Boil the eggs for 10 minutes.
2. Peel the eggs and cut them into thin slices as you like for a salad.
3. Coat the eggs with flour.
4. Cut the garlic and ginger into tiny pieces.
5. Add olive oil to a pan and cook over medium-high heat. Put in the eggs and fry them for 4 minutes.
6. Add the garlic, soy sauce, ginger, green onions, and chilies, and then cook for 3 more minutes. Keep mixing the ingredients.
7. Remove the eggs from the pan and serve.

_____ 1. Jamie is going to make golden coin eggs, and here is her shopping list. What did she forget to put on the list?

(A)

(B)

(C)

(D) ⬭

Shopping list
- ☐ eggs and flour
- ☐ green onions
- ☐ olive oil
- ☐ soy sauce
- ☐ ginger
- ☐ chili

_____ 2. Jamie would like to invite 5 friends to sample this dish. How many eggs does she need at least to make this recipe?

(A) Eight.　　　(B) Six.　　　(C) Five.　　　(D) Four.

Ⓐ Word Bank

1. spice up *phr.* 使……增添風味
2. serving [`sɝvɪŋ] *n.* [C] (供一人食用的) 一份
3. ginger [`dʒɪndʒɚ] *n.* [U] 薑
4. clove [klov] *n.* [C] 蒜瓣
5. garlic [`gɑrlɪk] *n.* [U] 大蒜
6. olive [`ɑlɪv] *n.* [C] 橄欖
7. chop [tʃɑp] *vt.* 剁碎
8. chili [`tʃɪlɪ] *n.* [C][U] 辣椒

✎ Practice　請將 Word Bank 中的單字填入空格，並依句意做出適當變化

1. I like dishes with many _____ in them. I really enjoy their hot and spicy taste.
2. It is said that _____ oil can help prevent heart disease.
3. George was so hungry that he ordered two _____ of spaghetti.
4. Some slices of _____ will give the fish soup a better flavor.
5. I helped my mom _____ some carrots to make vegetable soup.

Answer Key　1. chilies　2. olive　3. servings　4. ginger　5. chop

⑦ Pre-reading Questions

1. Have you ever played gachapon before? If yes, do you enjoy it?

2. Why do you play gachapon? Just for fun or to collect a specific toy?

📖 Target Vocabulary

vending machine *n.*
投幣式自動販賣機

crave *vt.*
渴望

manga *n.*
日本漫畫

specialty *n.*
名產

knob *n.*
旋鈕

🎁 Reading

Gachapon has been a fad① among Japanese youth for several decades. Gachapon is a tiny toys that pops② out of the vending machine③ in a clear plastic capsule④. The toys come in various sets, such as the manga⑤ characters and cute LINE characters. To get one, all you need to do is choose a machine that sells your preferred set, put the coins into the slot⑥, turn the knob⑦, and then wait for it to pop out!

Gachapon first appeared in Japan in 1965. With its low price and attractive design, it quickly caught children's eyes. Gachapon toys are perfect for playing, sharing, trading, or just collecting. To show off their collections, students like to hang them on their school bags or display them on their desks. Gachapon is said to be part of everyone's childhood memories. Not just for kids, gachapon toys are also loved by people of all ages.

Now, gachapon toys are more refined⑧ and better in quality, but they can also be more expensive than before. Where can you find gachapon machines? Besides the ordinary ones in convenience stores, customers can find specialty⑨ gachapon machines with amazing toys in appliance shops and novelty⑩ shops in Tokyo.

These fantastic gachapon toys add color to people's lives. Do you crave⑪ to own your gachapon? Pick one now!

_____ 1. Why did gachapon first become popular among children?

    (A) They liked to collect plastic capsules.

    (B) They enjoyed coloring toys.

    (C) They could get attractive toys at low price.

    (D) They envied the toys other classmates had.

_____ 2. Which of the following places is least likely to get a gachapon toy?

    (A) Appliance shops.   (B) Convenience stores.

    (C) Novelty shops.   (D) Farmer's markets.

_____ 3. What can people do with gachapon toys?

(A) They can collect a set of gachapon toys.

(B) They can exchange gachapon toys with others.

(C) They can play gachapon toys with other fans.

(D) All of the above.

🎯 After You Read

When did gachapon first appear in Japan?
It first appeared in Japan in 1965.

What is gachapon?
Gachapon is a tiny toy that pops out of the vending machine in a clear plastic capsule.

Where can people get a gachapon toy?
In convenience stores, appliance shops, and novelty shops in Tokyo.

What are the possible gachapon toys?
They come in various sets, such as the manga characters or cute LINE characters.

What can people do with gachapon toys?
They can play, share, trade, or just collect them.

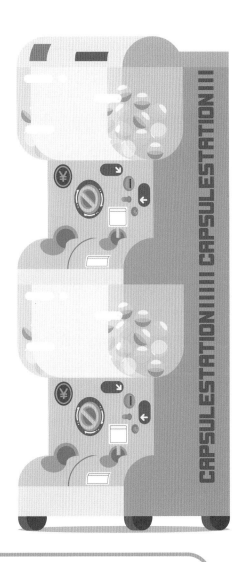

A Word Bank

1. fad [fæd] *n.* [C] 一時的流行
2. pop [pɑp] *vi.* (突然地) 出現
3. vending machine *n.* [C] 投幣式自動販賣機
4. capsule [`kæpsl̩] *n.* [C] 小容器
5. manga [`mæn,gə] *n.* [C] 日本漫畫
6. slot [slɑt] *n.* [C] 投幣口
7. knob [nɑb] *n.* [C] 旋鈕
8. refined [rɪ`faɪnd] *adj.* 精緻的
9. specialty [`spɛʃəltɪ] *n.* [C] 名產
10. novelty [`nɑvl̩tɪ] *n.* [U] 新奇
11. crave [krev] *vt.* 渴望

Practice 請將 Word Bank 中的單字填入空格，並依句意做出適當變化

1. Peter turned the volume _____ on the radio to make the music louder.

2. The ice cream is the _____ of the store. I highly recommend it to you.

3. Many pregnant women find them _____ food as their babies get bigger.

4. Ryan inserted a coin into the _____ of a payphone and dialed his home number.

5. Tina loved riding her new bicycle around, but the _____ wore off soon.

⑦ Pre-reading Questions

1. What is Ramadan?

2. Have you ever experienced fasting during Ramadan?

3. In Chinese culture, is there anything similar to Ramadan?

📖 Target Vocabulary

joyous *adj.*
高興的

Muslim *n.*
穆斯林

dusk *n.*
黃昏

spiritual *adj.*
心靈的

sermon *n.*
布道

🏛 Reading

Have you ever heard of Ramadan? It is one of the biggest events in the Islamic world. Muslims start the holy month of Ramadan in the ninth month of the Islamic calendar. Muslim families put up colorful decorations and lanterns on their walls to create a festive

atmosphere. Muslims also attend nightly prayer sessions, read the Quran, and think about the role of faith in their lives during the entire month of Ramadan.

During Ramadan, Muslims are required to fast from dawn until dusk. They are supposed to abstain from eating and drinking. Ramadan is intended to commemorate a miraculous event in Islam: Allah's revelation of the Quran to the Prophet Muhammad. Therefore, Muslims pursue spiritual renewal during the holy month. However, fasting is not just avoiding food and drink. It also includes avoiding bad conduct, such as gossiping, complaining, and smoking. The purpose of such fasting is to avoid hurting others with bad social habits. It also encourages self-awareness and kindness. Ramadan is a time to be a better person and to strengthen personal relationships.

"Eid al-Fitr" marks the end of the month of Ramadan. Starting with prayers, a short sermon, and gifts to charity, Eid al-Fitr is a joyous three-day holiday for Muslims. To celebrate, they would wear new clothes, give lucky money and treats to children, and visit friends, relatives, and graveyards. In short, it's a time to celebrate the Muslims' accomplishment of a month of fasting.

1. What is the passage mainly about?

(A) An introduction of an important Islamic custom.

(B) Religious teachings by the Prophet Muhammad.

(C) An inspiring story about self-improvement.

(D) A way to lose weight by fasting.

2. When is Ramadan?

(A) In every September.

(B) In the ninth month of the Islamic calendar.

(C) On the Prophet Muhammad's birthday.

(D) None of the above.

3. What is the purpose of fasting?

(A) To lose weight.

(B) To save money.

(C) To be a better person.

(D) To quit smoking.

4. Eid al-Fitr is _____ .

(A) a term to refer to Ramadan

(B) a religious text of Islam

(C) a holiday to end Ramadan

(D) a story in the Quran

5. During Ramadan, people avoid the following activities EXCEPT _____ .

(A) eating

(B) drinking

(C) smoking

(D) praying

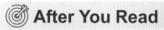 **After You Read**

Ramadar Kareem

What is Ramadan? And when is it?

It is the biggest event for Muslims to commemorate Allah's revelation of the Quran. It is in the ninth month of the Islamic calendar.

Activities during Ramadan: Dos and Don'ts

- Muslims attend nightly prayer sessions, read the Quran, and think about the role of faith in their lives.

- Muslims fast during Ramadan. Fasting is not just avoiding food and drink. It also includes avoiding bad conduct, such as gossiping, complaining, smoking, and losing your temper.

How long does Ramadan last?

One month. Then, Eid al-Fitr, a three-day holiday, marks the end of Ramadan.

A Word Bank

1. Ramadan [ˌræməˈdɑn] *n*. [U]
   齋月
2. Islamic [ɪzˈlæmɪk] *adj*. 伊斯蘭教的
3. Muslim [ˈmʌzlɪm] *n*. [C] 穆斯林；
   伊斯蘭教徒
4. festive [ˈfɛstɪv] *adj*. 節慶的
5. session [ˈsɛʃən] *n*. [C] (從事某項活動的) 一段時間
6. Quran [kəˈrɑn] *n*. [U] 《古蘭經》
7. fast [fæst] *vi*. 禁食；齋戒
8. dusk [dʌsk] *n*. [U] 黃昏
9. abstain [əbˈsten] *vi*. 節制

10. commemorate [kəˈmɛməˌret] *vt*.
    紀念
11. miraculous [məˈrækjələs] *adj*.
    奇蹟般的
12. revelation [ˌrɛvl̩ˈeʃən] *n*. [U][C]
    揭示
13. spiritual [ˈspɪrɪtʃuəl] *adj*. 心靈的
14. renewal [rɪˈnjuəl] *n*. [U][C] 恢復；
    更新
15. conduct [ˈkɑndʌkt] *n*. [U] 行為；
    舉止
16. sermon [ˈsɝmən] *n*. [C] 布道
17. joyous [ˈdʒɔɪəs] *adj*. 高興的

✎ Practice   請將 Word Bank 中的單字填入空格，並依句意做出適當變化

1. It was _____ that the three-year-old child did not get hurt when he fell off from the third floor.
2. The student's excellent _____ at school has made his parents very proud.
3. Reading the Bible always provides Melissa with _____ comfort.
4. Kelly had a(n) _____ family reunion on Christmas Eve. She enjoyed a relaxing atmosphere and feasted on homemade food.
5. We watched the beautiful sunset on the beach at _____.

 Answer Key   1. miraculous 2. conduct 3. spiritual 4. joyous 5. dusk

1. What is your favorite city in the world?

2. What things do you look forward to when you go on vacation?

3. What are things to consider when you plan a trip?

Target Vocabulary

wildlife *n.*
野生生物

scenery *n.*
風景

juggler *n.*
表演雜耍的人

massage *n.*
按摩

statue *n.*
雕像

Reading

Shoushan Zoo

Liuhe Night Market

Love River

Takao Railway Museum

Massage N' Café

The Pier-2 Art Center

When you visit Kaohsiung, you can start your trip at Love River. It's a romantic and perfect place to bring your date. The best way to appreciate Love River is to take a boat tour. Sitting in the boat, you can enjoy the beautiful scenery① and feel the nice breeze②. Also, make sure that you don't miss the Pier-2 Art Center, one of the most colorful spots in this city. You can appreciate installation art③ and murals④ created by the local artists and watch talented street performers like jugglers⑤ and living statues⑥ in action. Animal lovers should spend a few hours at Shoushan Zoo. You can see Formosan black bears, white rhinoceros⑦, and other wildlife⑧ with a reasonable⑨ entrance fee. For great food, Liuhe Night Market is your best choice. You can try lots of tasty snacks and do a little shopping there, too. When you're tired, head to Massage⑩ N' Café. You can get a massage while drinking a cup of coffee. What a great way to end your trip!

_____ 1. If you are an art lover, which of the following places should you pay a visit to?

    (A) Liuhe Night Market.   (B) Massage N' Café.

    (C) The Pier-2 Art Center.   (D) Shoushan Zoo.

_____ 2. Which of the following is **NOT** mentioned in the passage?

    (A) How to reach Kaohsiung from Taipei.

    (B) What you can admire during the boat tour at Love River.

    (C) Where you can find Formosan black bears.

    (D) Where to take a break and get a massage.

Ⓐ Word Bank

1. scenery [ˋsinərɪ] *n.* [U] 風景；景色
2. breeze [briz] *n.* [C] 微風
3. installation art *n.* [U] 裝置藝術
4. mural [ˋmjʊrəl] *n.* [C] 壁畫
5. juggler [ˋdʒʌglɚ] *n.* [C] 表演雜耍的人
6. statue [ˋstætʃu] *n.* [C] 雕像
7. rhinoceros [raɪˋnɑsərəs] *n.* [C] 犀牛
8. wildlife [ˋwaɪldˌlaɪf] *n.* [U] 野生生物
9. reasonable [ˋriznəbḷ] *adj.* 不貴的；價格公道的
10. massage [məˋsɑʒ] *n.* [U][C] 按摩

✎ Practice 請將 Word Bank 中的單字填入空格，並依句意做出適當變化

1. The poisonous chemicals will destroy plants and _____ in nature.
2. The government put up a life-size _____ of the great scientist in the park.
3. Helen rolled down the car window to enjoy the gentle _____ while driving.
4. The beautiful _____ of Orchid Island left a deep impression on the visitors.
5. My family enjoy dining at this seafood restaurant because it offers tasty food with _____ price.

Answer Key　1. wildlife　2. statue　3. breeze　4. scenery　5. reasonable

History
Intermediate Level

⑦ Pre-reading Questions

1. Do you know the origin of the marathon?
2. Have you ever participated in any marathon events?
3. What are the ways to train yourself to get ready for a marathon?
4. What is the secret to finishing a marathon?

📖 Target Vocabulary

fatigue *n.*
疲憊

exclaim *vi.*
呼喊

invade *vt.*
侵略

battlefield *n.*
戰場

collapse *vi.*
倒下

📖 Reading

What do you think of when you see the number 42.195? Well, the length of 42.195 kilometers① is the distance of a marathon race. However, have you ever wondered how people came to agree on the distance of a marathon?

About 2,500 years ago, the Persian king wanted to show off the empire's military strength, so he sent a huge army to invade② Athens. In order to get more help from other states, Athenians sent their best runner, Pheidippides, to Sparta. Pheidippides ran about 240 kilometers from Athens to Sparta in two days. However, the Spartans did not offer help as expected. As the enemy was approaching fast, Pheidippides could not afford to waste any time resting. Therefore, he ran back again.

Though Athens received very little support from other states, they faced the enemy bravely and finally won the battle. The battlefield③ was at Marathon, a town about 40 kilometers from Athens. Knowing that his people were anxious about the news of the battle, Pheidippides ran to spread the good news. The exertion④ of running hundreds of kilometers previous to the battle and then participating in the battle took its toll⑤ on his body. Nevertheless, Pheidippides was determined not to fail his country. Despite his fatigue⑥, he kept running.

Finally, he staggered⑦ through the city gate and collapsed⑧. "Rejoice, we conquer!" he exclaimed⑨ before taking his last breath. The Athenians were happy, but at the same time felt very sad about his death. Later, the marathon race was included in the Modern Olympic Games, and the distance was what Pheidippides had run. It is not just a race, but a tribute⑩ to this great runner, who bravely gave away his life for his countrymen⑪.

_____ 1. The best title for this passage can be "_____."

    (A) Marathons Around the World

    (B) How Athens Beat Sparta

    (C) The History of the Greek Empire

    (D) The Legend of the Marathon

2. Who was Pheidippides?

(A) He was a Persian king.　　(B) He was a terrific Athenian runner.

(C) He was a Greek athlete.　　(D) He was a brave Spartan general.

3. Which of the following is true about the marathon?

(A) It is a way to train a soldier's will and physical strength.

(B) It is the place to go before Athenians marched into the battlefield.

(C) It is a competition that dates back to 2,500 years ago.

(D) It is a tribute to Pheidippides, who gave away his life for the country.

◎ After You Read

The Origin of Marathon	
Setting (Where & When)	dates back 2,500 years
Character (Who)	Pheidippides, the best runner in Athens
Problem (Why)	The Persian king sent soldiers to fight Athens.
Action (What happened)	1. Pheidippides ran about 240 km to Sparta to get help, but in vain. 2. The war took place in Marathon, and it was about 40 km from Athens. 3. Athenians won the battle against the Persian army. 4. Pheidippides ran back to Athens to announce the victory and died of exhaustion.
Outcome (What happened)	To honor Pheidippides, the distance he ran from Marathon to Athens became the distance of the marathon.

A Word Bank

1. kilometer [`kɪlə,mitɚ] *n.* [C] 公里
2. invade [ɪn`ved] *vt.; vi.* 侵略
3. battlefield [`bætl̩,fild] *n.* [C] 戰場
4. exertion [ɪg`zɝʃən] *n.* [C][U]
   盡力；費力
5. take its/a toll *phr.* 造成損失
6. fatigue [fə`tig] *n.* [U] 疲憊
7. stagger [`stægɚ] *vi.* 蹣跚
8. collapse [kə`læps] *vi.* 倒下
9. exclaim [ɪk`sklem] *vi.* 呼喊
10. tribute [`trɪbjut] *n.* [C][U] 敬意
11. countryman [`kʌntrɪmən] *n.* [C]
    同胞

Practice 請將 Word Bank 中的單字填入空格，並依句意做出適當變化

1. "No way!" Susan _____ when she heard the news.
2. A marathon is a long-distance race which covers about 42 _____.
3. The audience was shocked when the stage _____.
4. Uncle Joe controlled the naughty boys with _____ so that they didn't spoil the family reunion.
5. The soldier fought bravely against the enemies on the _____.

? Pre-reading Questions

1. What is the story behind your name? Does it carry any significant meanings?

2. William Shakespeare once said, "A rose by any other name would smell as sweet." Does it make sense to you?

Aa Target Vocabulary

contract *n.*
合約

documentary *n.*
紀錄片

tedious *adj.*
單調乏味的

administrative *adj.*
行政的

document *n.*
文件

🎒 Reading

There is a movement toward aboriginal people in Taiwan starting to use their aboriginal names. The movement, as reported in the *Taipei Times*, has the support of famous celebrities on the island, such as the documentary① filmmaker Mayaw Biho.

Before 1995, aboriginal people needed to choose Chinese family names and first names on official documents②. These people were required by law to do so, until **it** was changed in 1995. Since then, aboriginal people have been able to change back to their original aboriginal names if they want to.

However, many aboriginal people have not undergone③ the process of changing their names, and they have different reasons for not doing so. First of all, making the change can be a difficult process. To begin the process, they have to deal with tedious④ paperwork at the local household registration office. Most of them are not willing to spend time doing so. In addition, this is only the first step in the process. What follows is the need to make changes on all other official documents and contracts⑤. This can mean changing passports, phone contracts, and many other agreements where a Chinese identification card is used to establish identity.

Aside from⑥ complicated administrative⑦ work, some aboriginal people fear they may face discrimination by non-aboriginal people. However, the aboriginal names given to them have cultural significance. These names would serve as a bridge connecting the aboriginal people with their history. Some even believe that keeping the aboriginal name can help bring the people closer to the cultures of their tribes.

Currently, there are about half a million aboriginal people living on the island. Out of this number, only about 20,000 of them have chosen to go back to their tribal names. If the movement catches on⑧, the number could increase greatly in the future.

1. According to the passage, what is true about Mayaw Biho?

   (A) He wrote many articles on aboriginal people for the *Taipei Times*.

   (B) He supported the movement of the return to aboriginal names.

   (C) He criticized the movement of the return to aboriginal names.

   (D) He was the first aboriginal person to give up his Chinese name.

2. Which of the following is **NOT** mentioned in the name-changing process?

   (A) Posting the name-changing results in the *Taipei Times*.

   (B) Applying for the process at the household registration office.

   (C) Changing the name back to the original aboriginal name.

   (D) Making a change on other official documents as well.

3. What does the word "**it**" refer to in the second paragraph?

   (A) The law to choose Chinese family names.

   (B) The law to change back to aboriginal names.

   (C) The movement to keep aboriginal names.

   (D) The movement to use Chinese names.

4. According to the passage, which of the following is true?

   (A) The *Taipei Times* is leading the movement of the return to tribal names.

   (B) The year 1995 is an important year for aboriginal people.

   (C) There are only 20,000 aboriginal people living in Taiwan.

   (D) Processing paperwork to change the name is expensive.

5. What makes the aboriginal people hesitate to change back to their original aboriginal names?

   (A) They think the name-changing process is a waste of money.

   (B) They want to honor their Chinese names.

   (C) They don't want to be closer to the cultures of their tribes.

   (D) They are worried about being discriminated against after they change their names.

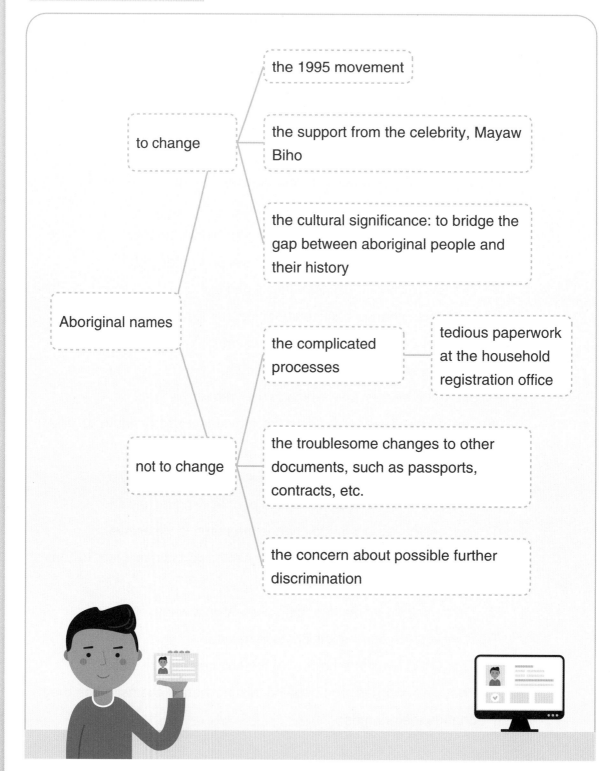

the 1995 movement

the support from the celebrity, Mayaw Biho

to change

the cultural significance: to bridge the gap between aboriginal people and their history

Aboriginal names

the complicated processes

tedious paperwork at the household registration office

not to change

the troublesome changes to other documents, such as passports, contracts, etc.

the concern about possible further discrimination

Ⓐ Word Bank

1. documentary [͵dɑkjə`mɛntərɪ] *n.* [C] 紀錄片
2. document [`dɑkjəmənt] *n.* [C] 文件
3. undergo [͵ʌndɚ`go] *vt.* 經歷
4. tedious [`tidɪəs] *adj.* 冗長乏味的
5. contract [`kɑntrækt] *n.* [C] 合約
6. aside from *phr.* 除⋯⋯之外
7. administrative [əd`mɪnə͵stretɪv] *adj.* 行政的
8. catch on *phr.* 變得流行

✐ Practice   請將 Word Bank 中的單字填入空格，並依句意做出適當變化

1. You must check every single detail of the _____ before putting your signature to it.
2. The speaker bored the listeners with the _____ details of his research.
3. The cancer patient _____ major surgery to remove his brain tumor.
4. Tony works as a(n) _____ assistant. He is responsible for organizing the work of the sales department.
5. The director made this _____ to raise people's awareness of the aboriginal people's rights.

⑦ Pre-reading Questions

1. Do you like watching basketball games? Which team do you support?

2. Can you name a few basketball players that you support?

3. How much do you know about the terms and positions in basketball?

🔠 Target Vocabulary

knight *n.*
騎士

dunk *vt.*
灌籃

stats *n.*
統計數字

line-up *n.*
陣容

summary *n.*
總結

 Reading

This is Todd Rocker reporting with SSPN. Ladies and gentlemen, hold on to your seats. Tonight's game between the NY Knights① and the LA Runners was one of the year's best. The Knights got off to a fast start, and you couldn't miss its star power forward②, Karl Jones. He scored 20 points in the third quarter. The Runners wouldn't quit though. Donnie Lee was on fire in the fourth quarter. He had a 3-point shot with 7 seconds left to tie③ the game. On the last play of the game, the Knights' center, Ollie Kenyata, got open and dunked④ right before the end of the game. It was amazing! We've never seen Kenyata play like this before. Here is the summary⑤ of the stats⑥.

Game Date: September 22, 2018—8:00 p.m. Eastern Time (ET)

Top Scorers⑦:

| NYK-Karl Jones-37 points | LAR-Donnie Lee-45 points |

	1	2	3	4	T
NYK	27	23	34	35	119
LAR	31	23	24	39	117

Starting Line-ups⑧

NY Knights		LA Runners
Ollie Kenyata	Center	Vadim Putin
Karl Jones	Power Forward (PF)	Ruben Marks
Ron Barks	Small Forward (SF)	Eric Azalea
Paul Euler	Point Guard⑨ (PG)	Kobe Shinobe
Darren Paso	Shooting Guard (SG)	Donnie Lee

_____ 1. Why was Ollie Kenyata so amazing in the game?

(A) He scored 20 points in the third quarter.

(B) He was a power forward for NYK.

(C) He had a 3-point shot with 7 seconds left in the game.

(D) He dunked right before the game was over.

_____ 2. Which of the following is true about the game?

(A) The top scorer of LAR scored more than that of NYK.

(B) The game finally ended in a tie.

(C) Todd Rocker is the spokesperson for both teams.

(D) It usually takes 7 seconds to have a 3-point shot in one game.

Ⓐ Word Bank

1. knight [naɪt] *n.* [C] 騎士
2. forward [`fɔrwəd] *n.* [C] 前鋒
3. tie [taɪ] *vt.* 不分勝負
4. dunk [dʌŋk] *vi.* 灌籃
5. summary [`sʌmərɪ] *n.* [C] 總結

6. stats [stæts] *n.* [plural] 統計數字
7. scorer [`skɔrə] *n.* [C] 得分者
8. line-up [`laɪn,ʌp] *n.* [C] 陣容
9. guard [gɑrd] *n.* [C] 後衛

✏ Practice 請將 Word Bank 中的單字填入空格，並依句意做出適當變化

1. The _____ show that more and more people nowadays are addicted to their smartphones.

2. Because of the serious knee injury, Charlie was not in the starting _____ of tonight's game.

3. At the end of the game, we were _____ with our competitor.

4. To improve our reading and writing skills, our teacher always asks us to write a(n) _____ after we finish reading an article.

5. The _____ are allowed to carry swords around the king.

Sport
Intermediate Level

⑦ Pre-reading Questions

1. What do you know about South Korea?

2. In your opinion, what do people often associate South Korea with?

3. Have you ever played e-sports?

4. What makes people indulge themselves in playing e-sports?

📖 Target Vocabulary

contest *n.*
比賽

commitment *n.*
投入

stadium *n.*
體育場

high-tech *adj.*
高科技的

endorse *vt.*
宣傳

🎮 Reading

South Korea is one of Asia's leading sporting nations. Its baseball and soccer teams have long been ranked as one of the best around the world. In addition, when it comes to e-sports (also known as electronic sports or video gaming), people will not miss South Korea.

Millions of people in South Korea regularly play e-sports. The country also has professional e-sports leagues① and a series of big-money competitions. Many of these contests② are held in large stadiums③ with tens of thousands of fans **rooting for** their favorite teams.

With so much interest in these events, the life of a top e-sports player is fairly similar to that of other sports stars. They usually spend 12 hours a day practicing playing to improve their gaming skills. As they become famous, they have sponsors paying them to endorse④ items of clothing and high-tech⑤ products. It's not rare for them to earn a large amount of money. However, life of the e-sports players is not as colorful as it appears. Even though it might sound like an easy job, these players actually train very hard.

Being good at video games isn't enough to get to the top. It takes hard work and real dedication⑥. For most people, this level of commitment⑦ is too much, and they just play games for fun. What about you? Do you think you have what it takes to get to the top of the e-sports world?

_____ 1. The phrase "**rooting for**" in the second paragraph is the closest to

_____.

　　(A) watching　　(B) fighting　　(C) staying　　(D) supporting

_____ 2. What is **NOT** true about the life of e-sports players?

　　(A) They train very hard.

　　(B) They play games just for fun.

　　(C) Most of them are from South Korea.

　　(D) Most of them belong to leagues.

_____ 3. According to the passage, what might attract people most to dedicate themselves to e-sports?

(A) Money and fame.   (B) Sponsors and trips.

(C) Clothing and fun.   (D) Exercise and gaming skills.

 **After You Read**

When it comes to e-sports, people will not miss South Korea.

South Korea has professional e-sports leagues.

As an e-sports player becomes famous, sponsors would pay him or her to endorse items of clothing and high-tech products.

An e-sports player needs to spend 12 hours a day or more practicing playing to improve his or her gaming skills, just like other sports stars.

The contestants may win big money in those competitions.

It might sound like an easy job to be an e-sports player; however, it takes hard work and real dedication.

Ⓐ Word Bank

1. league [lig] *n.* [C] 聯盟
2. contest [`kɑntɛst] *n.* [C] 比賽
3. stadium [`stediəm] *n.* [C] 體育場
4. endorse [ɪn`dɔrs] *vt.* 宣傳
5. high-tech [`haɪ`tɛk] *adj.* 高科技的
6. dedication [͵dɛdə`keʃən] *n.* [U] 奉獻
7. commitment [kə`mɪtmənt] *n.* [C][U] 投入

✎ Practice　請將 Word Bank 中的單字填入空格，並依句意做出適當變化

1. The winner of this singing _____ will get a contract to release an album.
2. Thanks to the _____ of the doctor, the patient recovered from his illness quickly.
3. The actor will not _____ a product unless he has used it. He only recommends something he is satisfied with.
4. That basketball team, which belongs to the national _____, is expected to win this year's championship.
5. _____ devices, such as smartphones and tablet computers, have completely changed people's lives.

⑦ Pre-reading Questions

1. How much do you know about soldiers performing military drill?

2. On what occasion can you see soldiers performing military drill?

🔤 Target Vocabulary

rifle *n.*
步槍

blindfold *n.*
眼罩

drill *n.*
軍事訓練

in formation *phr.*
編隊

march *vi.*
行軍

🎒 Reading

In May 2018, the World Drill① Championships (WDC) took place in Daytona Beach, Florida. As reported in the *Liberty Times*, a member of the Taiwan Navy Honor Guard named Su Chi-lin took fourth place. Along with this, he also won a special founder's② award.

He was competing against 35 contestants, and he demonstrated excellent skills in handling a rifle③. As the first soldier from Taiwan's military to compete in the WDC, Su became the pride of Taiwan.

As part of military training, all soldiers must practice military drill to learn to march④ in formation⑤. The origin of the military drill was for a simple reason—commanders⑥ needed a way to move large numbers of soldiers, and these soldiers often had to march long distances.

When marching into the battlefield, separate groups of soldiers would often end up gathering in the same area. By training soldiers to march as large groups, commanders could minimize⑦ the risk of soldiers getting lost. After doing months of marching drills, the soldiers could be kept together and thus commanded as a group. Today, military drill is not just about marching. It also includes special rifle-handling skills that are performed when the troops⑧ are presented on national holidays.

In the WDC, Su Chi-lin was cheered by the crowd when he performed his solo military drill. To show how well he could do with his rifle, he even performed part of his routine by wearing a blindfold⑨. Upon finishing, he yelled, "Thank you, WDC! Thank you, America! I love you, Taiwan!"

_____ 1. What is the best title for this passage?

(A) A Special Report of the WDC

(B) How to Handle a Rifle

(C) The History of Military Drill

(D) The Pride of Taiwan

_____ 2. What makes Su Chi-lin so special in the WDC?

(A) He is a sailor based in Florida.

(B) He is the first Taiwanese to compete in the WDC.

(C) He is good at commanding soldiers to march.

(D) He is the first Taiwanese commander in the US Navy.

_____ 3. According to the passage, what is the purpose of marching?

(A) To pass the time.

(B) To make the enemy angry.

(C) To entertain commanders.

(D) To move around effectively.

_____ 4. Why did Su wear a blindfold in the performance?

(A) To meet the requirement of the WDC.

(B) To protect his eyes from possible harm.

(C) To avoid distractions from the crowd.

(D) To show his skills in handling a rifle.

_____ 5. Based on the passage, which of the following is true?

(A) The WDC is an annual event in Taiwan.

(B) It is necessary for commanders to join the WDC.

(C) Marching in formation is equally important for commanders and
soldiers.

(D) Taiwan always impresses the world in the WDC.

As a part of military training, military drill makes soldiers learn to march in formation into the battlefield.

Today, military drill is not just about marching. It also includes special rifle-handling skills.

Su Chi-lin was the first soldier from Taiwan's military to compete in the WDC.

Su Chi-lin took fourth place in the 2018 World Drill Championships and became the pride of Taiwan.

Su Chi-lin was cheered by the crowd when he performed part of his routine by wearing a blindfold in the contest.

Ⓐ Word Bank

1. drill [drɪl] *n.* [U][C] (尤指軍事) 訓練
2. founder [`faʊndɚ] *n.* [C] 創辦人
3. rifle [`raɪfḷ] *n.* [C] 步槍；來福槍
4. march [mɑrtʃ] *vi.; vt.* 行軍
5. in formation *phr.* 編隊
6. commander [kə`mændɚ] *n.* [C] 指揮官
7. minimize [`mɪnə,maɪz] *vt.* 使……降到最低限度
8. troops [trups] *n.* [plural] 部隊
9. blindfold [`blaɪnd,fold] *n.* [C] 眼罩

✎ **Practice** 請將 Word Bank 中的單字填入空格，並依句意做出適當變化

1. On Double Tenth Day, soldiers will ＿＿＿＿ down the streets in front of the Presidential Office Building to celebrate the national day of Taiwan.
2. With his ＿＿＿＿, the hunter fired a shot at the deer.
3. Mark Zuckerberg is known as the ＿＿＿＿ and CEO of the famous social networking website, Facebook.
4. In order to ＿＿＿＿ the risk of being stolen, Jeff stored all of his valuables in the safe.
5. In the peace talks, the two opposing countries reached an agreement to withdraw both of their ＿＿＿＿.

Unit 9 運動 Sport

Unit 10

Health Care
Basic Level

1. Do you know how to read a doctor's prescription?

2. Are you allergic to any medicines? Why is it important to know?

Target Vocabulary

consulting *adj.*
提供諮詢的

dosage *n.*
劑量

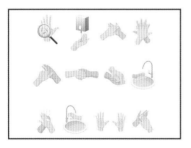

precaution *n.*
預防措施

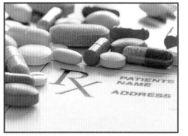

prescription *n.*
處方

vomit *vi.*
嘔吐

 **Reading**

Helen has been sick for several days. She had a high fever and even vomited① this morning. Therefore, Helen made an appointment to see the doctor. The doctor wrote her this prescription②.

FAMILY CLINIC③

No. 123, Fuxing N. Rd., Zhongshan Dist., Taipei City 104, Taiwan (R.O.C.)
TEL: (02) 2234-1234
Consulting④ Hours: Monday thru Saturday   09:00 a.m.～10:00 p.m.

Date: 07/25/2018   **Medical Record No.:** 000001   **Prescription No.:** B0001

Name: Helen Conroy   **Gender/Age:** Female/25   **Appointment No.:** 1234567

Administration⑤ and Dosage⑥: [Oral] For each medicine, take one tablet after each

meal.

Duration⑦: 3 days

Drug Name:

Acetaminophen 500 mg tablet

Domperidone 10 mg tablet

IWELL tablet

Precautions⑧:

Avoid alcohol while taking the medicine.

Physician: *Mike Lawrence*

_____ 1. Which of the following statements about Helen is **NOT** true?

    (A) Her family name is Lawrence.

    (B) She is 25 years old now.

    (C) July 25, 2018 is the date she saw the doctor.

    (D) Helen has been feeling ill for more than one day.

_____ 2. Which of the following statements is true?

    (A) Helen has to take the medicine before every meal.

    (B) The Family Clinic opens every day.

    (C) Mike Lawrence works at the Family Clinic.

    (D) The Family Clinic is located in New Taipei City.

Ⓐ Word Bank

1. vomit [ˋvɑmɪt] *vi.* 嘔吐
2. prescription [prɪˋskrɪpʃən] *n.* [C] 處方
3. clinic [ˋklɪnɪk] *n.* [C] 診所
4. consulting [kənˋsʌltɪŋ] *adj.* 提供諮詢的
5. administration [ədˏmɪnəˋstreʃən] *n.* [U] 施用
6. dosage [ˋdosɪdʒ] *n.* [C] 劑量
7. duration [djuˋreʃən] *n.* [U] 持續時間
8. precaution [prɪˋkɔʃən] *n.* [C] 預防措施

✏ Practice 　請將 Word Bank 中的單字填入空格，並依句意做出適當變化

1. The _____ of today's speech is two hours, and refreshments will be served afterward.

2. The bad smell was so disgusting that it made Ken _____.

3. My grandmother told the doctor to reduce her daily _____ because she was bothered by the side effect of the medicine.

4. Without the doctor's _____, you cannot buy this medicine.

5. This _____ company provides information for people who want to study abroad.

Unit 10

Health Care
Intermediate Level

⑦ Pre-reading Questions

1. Do you often eat out or eat at home?

2. Do you exercise regularly? How often do you exercise?

3. How much time do you spend commuting daily?

4. Do you consider yourself to be healthy?

🔠 Target Vocabulary

cycle *vi.*
騎腳踏車

affluence *n.*
富裕

hopeless *adj.*
絕望的

addictive *adj.*
使人上癮的

commute *vi.*
通勤

📖 Reading

Despite the advances we have made in technology and medical treatment, modern life is not at all conducive① to good health. Many of us work long hours and spend a lot of time commuting②. That leaves us with limited time and energy to make healthy meals or get exercise. In addition, the addictive③ nature of smartphones cause people to stay awake at night and check their phones when it is supposed to be time to sleep.

All these unhealthy lifestyles are eating away at our health. Research indicates that most of us are suffering from serious health conditions, such as diabetes④, heart disease, and depression. Although these health problems can be caused by other factors, medical experts assert⑤ that our unhealthy lifestyle is the major cause. Reading this, you might feel your future looks pretty hopeless⑥, but that doesn't have to be the case. You can combat⑦ these modern health problems, so-called "diseases of affluence⑧," by following the tips below.

First of all, eat healthily. Eat as much fresh fruit and vegetables as you can. Avoid food that is too greasy⑨ or overly processed⑩. If possible, you should lower the frequency of having instant noodles and pre-prepared meals. Second, exercise regularly. Try cycling⑪, swimming, or a fun sport with friends. Find out one sport you like, and do it regularly! Finally, take care of your mental health by spending time with friends and family, and get enough sleep at night. These things might not be easy to follow, but they'll make your life healthier, happier, and longer.

_____ 1. What is the best title for this passage?

    (A) Lifestyles in Developing Countries

    (B) Preventing Diseases of Affluence

    (C) How to Relieve Your Stress

    (D) 20 Ways to Improve Your Health

_____ 2. Which of the following does **NOT** improve our health?

    (A) Exercising regularly.   (B) Eating more fresh food.

     3. Which of the following statements is **NOT** mentioned in the passage?

       (A) Avoiding pre-prepared meals is good for your health.

       (B) Keeping in touch with friends is a way to relieve stress.

       (C) Poor people would face diseases of affluence as well.

       (D) Modern health problems will not be improved unless you change your lifestyle.

◎ After You Read

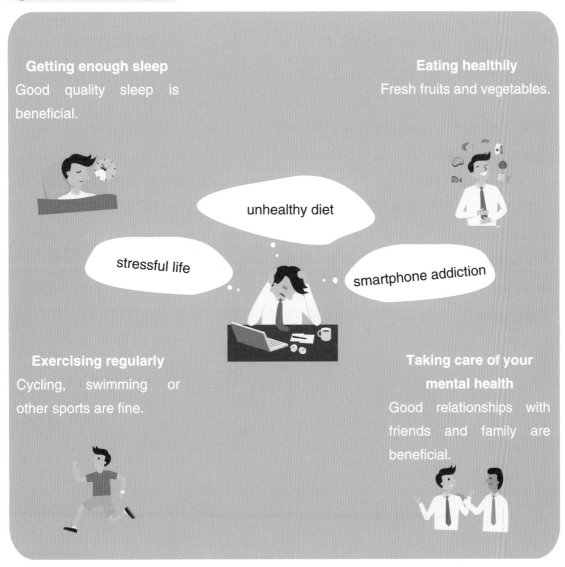

Getting enough sleep
Good quality sleep is beneficial.

Eating healthily
Fresh fruits and vegetables.

unhealthy diet

stressful life

smartphone addiction

Exercising regularly
Cycling, swimming or other sports are fine.

Taking care of your mental health
Good relationships with friends and family are beneficial.

Unit 10 醫療 Health Care

A Word Bank

1. conducive [kən`djusɪv] *adj.* 有益的
2. commute [kə`mjut] *vi.* 通勤
3. addictive [ə`dɪktɪv] *adj.* 使人上癮的
4. diabetes [͵daɪə`bitɪs] *n.* [U] 糖尿病
5. assert [ə`sɝt] *vt.* 主張

6. hopeless [`hoplɪs] *adj.* 絕望的
7. combat [`kɑmbæt] *vt.* 制止；打擊
8. affluence [`æfluəns] *n.* [U] 富裕
9. greasy [`grisɪ] *adj.* 油膩的
10. processed [`prɑsɛst] *adj.* 加工過的
11. cycle [`saɪkḷ] *vi.* 騎腳踏車

Practice 請將 Word Bank 中的單字填入空格，並依句意做出適當變化

1. Thanks to the high-speed rail, more and more people choose to _____ from their homes to their offices in faraway places.

2. According to a study, using a smartphone for a long time is not _____ to your vision.

3. Caffeine can be _____, which means that a person may need it badly and not be able to quit it.

4. Governments around the world must seek ways to _____ global warming and reduce its impact on the environment.

5. The suspect _____ his innocence, saying that he was not involved in the crime.

⑦ Pre-reading Questions

1. Do you know the novel *Frankenstein*? What is the story about?

2. Can you give some examples of how science has improved our lives?

3. What are some problems people may face when pursuing the advancement of science?

📖 Target Vocabulary

ponder *vi.*
沉思

pesticide *n.*
殺蟲劑

disapprove *vi.*
反對

breakthrough *n.*
重大進展

clone *n.*
無性繁殖

🏠 Reading

Frankenstein is one of the classics that is still relevant① today because it makes us to ponder② over the relationship between science and ethics③. For example, many people disapprove④ of animal testing, believing it to be

cruel and painful to those helpless creatures. Although many medical breakthroughs⑤ have benefited from animal testing, we still can't take it for granted. The question is how much greater human beings are compared to other animals, and whether those animals deserve rights and protections.

Another case that may cross ethical boundaries⑥ is GM foods. Nowadays, many crops are genetically modified, so they won't be harmed by certain herbicides⑦ and pesticides⑧. For farmers, these crops are easy to grow and fast to harvest. Yet, over the long term, will side effects such as "superweeds" cause more harm than good? Still, another issue related to the genetic engineering needs to be addressed. In 1996, scientists already have the skills to create a clone⑨ using the cell from an adult sheep. Currently, we may not yet be ready to make a human clone, but genetic testing is widely practiced for parents-to-be to screen out fetuses⑩ with genetic disorders. Although this helps parents-to-be be more prepared before childbirth, some argue that it may contribute to more abortions⑪.

Today, science and ethics are woven together in such a way that there will always be arguments. Rather than become easier to be solved, though, this problem will only continue to get more difficult.

_____ 1. What is the main idea of this passage?

(A) *Frankenstein* is a novel that all scientists should read.

(B) Animal testing is cruel, and we should stop it.

(C) Genetic engineering is beneficial to humans.

(D) Science develops, but ethical problems might follow.

_____ 2. According to the passage, what is **NOT** the feature of GM foods?

(A) GM foods taste more delicious.

(B) The crops of GM foods grow faster.

(C) The plants of GM foods are tougher.

(D) GM foods are easy to cultivate for farmers.

_____ 3. The sheep clone is groundbreaking because it is created out of the _____ of the sheep.

(A) weed   (B) fetus   (C) cell   (D) skin

_____ 4. The controversial examples between science and ethics are discussed in the passage, EXCEPT _____ .

(A) the cruelty of animal testing

(B) the evolution of superweeds

(C) the genetic testing of fetuses

(D) the abortion of the disordered clone

_____ 5. What is the author's attitude toward the future relationship between science and ethics?

(A) It will maintain the status quo.

(B) It will be no more problems.

(C) It will be more complicated.

(D) It will be very predictable.

🎯 After You Read

Two main issues raised from the novel *Frankenstein*

Science

Ethics

Animal Testing
medical advancements

Animal Testing
cruelty and pain to animals

GM Foods
1. high herbicide and pesticide resistance
2. fast growth and better harvest

GM Foods
unknown long-term side effects on humans and the environment

Genetic Engineering
eugenics

Genetic Engineering
illegal abortions

Ⓐ Word Bank

1. relevant [ˈrɛləvənt] *adj.* 有關的
2. ponder [ˈpɑndɚ] *vi.* 沉思
3. ethics [ˈɛθɪks] *n.* [U] 倫理學
4. disapprove [ˌdɪsəˈpruv] *vi.* 反對
5. breakthrough [ˈbrekˌθru] *n.* [C] 重大進展；突破
6. boundary [ˈbaʊndərɪ] *n.* [C] 界線
7. herbicide [ˈhɝˌbɪsaɪd] *n.* [C] 除草劑
8. pesticide [ˈpɛstɪsaɪd] *n.* [C] 殺蟲劑
9. clone [klon] *n.* [C] (動植物的) 無性繁殖
10. fetus [ˈfitəs] *n.* [C] 胎兒
11. abortion [əˈbɔrʃən] *n.* [C] 墮胎；人工流產

✎ Practice 請將 Word Bank 中的單字填入空格，並依句意做出適當變化

1. After a one-month investigation, the police finally announced a major _____ in the murder case.

2. The farmer sprayed _____ in the field to prevent his crops from being eaten up by bugs.

3. When the doctor told Jasmine that a(n) _____ was her only choice to save her own life, she cried sadly as she did not want to lose the baby.

4. Even though Peggy's parents _____ of her relationship with Ivan, she decided to get engaged to him.

5. I regret going to the movies because I was fooled by the title of the film. The name is absolutely not _____ to the story of the movie.

Unit 10 醫療 Health Care

Unit 11

Travel
Basic Level

⑦ Pre-reading Questions

1. Which country will be your first choice if you have a chance to travel abroad?

2. What are the things you have in mind when it comes to deciding a travel destination?

🔠 Target Vocabulary

destination *n.*
目的地

departure *n.*
啟程

suitcase *n.*
手提箱

set off *phr.*
出發

ground staff *n.*
地勤人員

🎒 Reading

It is Tara's first time traveling abroad. Before she booked the flight, she took many cities into consideration. For example, her dream was to visit the Eiffel Tower and have a cup of coffee at the Left Bank in Paris, but the tickets and other expenses were beyond her budget. Many of her friends also recommended her to visit Bangkok, but Tara was not into① beaches and hot weather at all. Finally, she chose Tokyo as her destination since she was fond of Japanese food and culture. Tara finished packing her suitcase② the night before departure③ and set off④ for the airport early in the morning.

At the airport, the ground staff⑤ helped her check in her luggage⑥ and gave her the boarding pass. Now she is checking her flight information before heading for the gate.

Airline	Flight No.	Destination⑦	Departure Time	Gate	Status⑧
Yellow Airlines	TG–123	Bangkok	8:30 a.m.	D3	Delayed
Purple Airlines	JL–428	Tokyo	10:00 a.m.	B4	On Time
Red Airlines	CI–724	Paris	10:25 a.m.	A7	Cancelled

✈ **Purple Airlines** | **Economy Class** | Gate **B4**

Name
Tara Smith

Taipei → Tokyo

JL-428 | 10:00 | 14 JUL

| Boarding Time | Zone | Seat |
| 9:30 | C | 20B |

Gate
B4

Tokyo
Taipei
14 JUL
10:00
Seat 20B
Zone C
Name Tara Smith
JL-428
Boarding Time 9:30

_____ 1. Which boarding gate should Tara go to?

(A) D3.　　　　(B) B4.　　　　(C) A7.　　　　(D) T1.

_____ 2. What will Tara probably enjoy most in this trip?

(A) Cruising on a whale-watching boat.

(B) Going sightseeing around the Eiffel Tower.

(C) Sunbathing on the beach and having a cold drink.

(D) Visiting the Tokyo Skytree and having some delicious Japanese food.

Ⓐ Word Bank

1. be into *phr.* 對……很有興趣
2. suitcase [`sut,kes] *n.* [C] (旅行用的) 手提箱
3. departure [dɪ`partʃɚ] *n.* [C] 啟程
4. set off *phr.* 出發
5. ground staff *n.* [C] 地勤人員
6. luggage [`lʌgɪdʒ] *n.* [U] 行李
7. destination [,dɛstə`neʃən] *n.* [C] 目的地
8. status [`stetəs] *n.* [C] 狀態

✎ Practice　請將 Word Bank 中的單字填入空格，並依句意做出適當變化

1. Bus drivers have the responsibility to transport passengers to their _____ safely.
2. Many people will carry _____ while traveling abroad.
3. There is a timetable showing arrivals and _____ of trains on the platform.
4. Tom is really _____ singing, so he always goes to karaoke with his friends.
5. After breakfast, the couple checked out of the hotel and _____ off for the last stop of their journey.

⑦ Pre-reading Questions

1. Do you prefer traveling alone or with a group?

2. Have you ever been to Japan? What's your impression of Japan?

🔠 Target Vocabulary

booklet *n.*
小冊子

indoor *adj.*
室內的

Buddhist *adj.*
佛教的

lobby *n.*
大廳

souvenir *n.*
紀念品

🔔 Reading

During my trip to Tokyo, I decided to visit one of the city's most famous buildings: Tokyo Skytree. Its height of 634 meters has so far made it the tallest tower in the world. Many Japanese television companies broadcast their signals from the tower, instead of the old Tokyo Tower. Additionally, it's also a major tourist attraction that offers a great view of Tokyo.

When I saw Tokyo Skytree from the ground, I was so impressed by its design. It looked like a high-tech tree that came from the future. When I walked in the lobby①, I was surprised by the indoor② facilities. Visitors can grab a cup of coffee at Skytree Café, buy some souvenirs③ at Skytree Shop, or enjoy a delicious meal at Sky Restaurant.

I spent some time reading the Tokyo Skytree tourist booklet④ before I came here. The Tembo Galleria was the place I really wanted to visit. After buying the ticket, I quickly took the elevator to the Tembo Galleria. As I stepped out of the elevator, the panoramic⑤ view of the city was in front of me. Landmarks⑥ like Sensoji, an ancient Buddhist⑦ temple, and Mt. Fuji could be spotted at once. I also saw the busy streets through the glass floor, and that was a really interesting and amazing experience. Tokyo Skytree is definitely one of my favorite places in Japan. So, if you have the chance to travel to Tokyo, I highly recommend visiting Tokyo Skytree.

_____ 1. If you want to get a panoramic view of Tokyo, you should go to
_____ in Tokyo Skytree.
  (A) Sensoji (B) Mt. Fuji
  (C) Skytree Shop (D) Tembo Galleria

_____ 2. Which of the following is **NOT** the feature of Tokyo Skytree?
  (A) It looks like a high-tech tree.
  (B) Its height is 634 meters.
  (C) Shopping is not allowed there.
  (D) TV companies broadcast from there.

_____ 3. What's the author's feeling about this trip to Tokyo Skytree?

(A) Bitter and disgusted.　　　　(B) Impressed and delighted.

(C) Sad and nostalgic.　　　　　(D) Shocked and scared.

After You Read

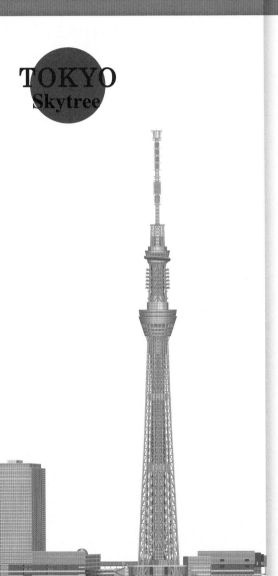

★ **Height:** Tokyo Skytree reaches a full height of 634 meters.

★ **Significance:** Tokyo Skytree is the tallest tower in the world.

★ **Function:** Tokyo Skytree is a broadcasting and communication tower. It also serves as a major tourist attraction.

★ **Design:** It looks like a high-tech tree from the future.

★ **Facilities:** Skytree Café, Skytree Shop, Sky Restaurant, and the Tembo Galleria.

A Word Bank

1. lobby [`lɑbɪ] *n.* [C] 大廳
2. indoor [ɪn`dor] *adj.* 室內的
3. souvenir [ˌsuvə`nɪr] *n.* [C] 紀念品
4. booklet [`bʊklɪt] *n.* [C] 小冊子
5. panoramic [ˌpænə`ræmɪk] *adj.* 全景的
6. landmark [`lænd,mɑrk] *n.* [C] 地標
7. Buddhist [`bʊdɪst] *adj.* 佛教的

✎ Practice   請將 Word Bank 中的單字填入空格，並依句意做出適當變化

1. Every time I go traveling abroad, I spend quite a lot of money buying _____ for my family and friends.
2. The new skyscraper has become a famous _____. Many tourists visit here when they come to the city.
3. This _____ contains all the information about this tourist attraction.
4. In Taiwan, _____ smoking is forbidden. Anyone who violates the rule will be fined.
5. I was first attracted to the crystal chandelier hanging from the ceiling when I entered the _____ of the hotel.

Unit 11

Travel
Advanced Level

⑦ Pre-reading Questions

1. On what occasions do people leave tips?

2. How much will you tip if you are satisfied with the service?

🔤 Target Vocabulary

mandatory *adj.*
強制的

gratitude *n.*
感謝

gratuity *n.*
小費

starting point *n.*
起點

bewildering *adj.*
困惑的

📖 Reading

Imagine enjoying a delicious dinner at a fancy restaurant in a foreign country. Everything is perfect until the waiter hands you the check. All of a sudden①, you realize that you have no idea whether you should tip or not!

Giving gratuities② is a common way to express your gratitude③ by leaving a small amount of money for someone who has offered a service to you. In Taiwan, tipping is not customary④, but views on leaving tips are a bit different worldwide. For example, in France, restaurants usually include a service fee in the bill, and thus it's not necessary to leave a tip. However, the French word for "tip" is "pourboire," which means "to have a drink." Therefore, French people consider tipping a friendly way to buy your waiter a glass of wine for a job well done.

When in Rome, you're supposed to do as the Romans do. When it comes to tipping though, it's a bit bewildering⑤. Tips aren't mandatory⑥ in Italy, but people often leave small tips if they can afford them. As for the United States, it is presumably⑦ the tipping capital of the world. Besides restaurants, people leave tips at bars, in taxis, and many other places because people in the service industry are not paid a lot. To leave a tip, some people would double the tax, while others would add 15 to 20 percent of the total bill. Whatever you do, be sure to leave something, otherwise people will think you are **boorish**.

These tipping tips are just a starting point⑧ though. Before you visit a foreign country, try to spend a little time researching its tipping culture. In this way, you can avoid some embarrassing situations while traveling.

1. Where would you probably read about this passage?

   (A) A section in a travel guide.

   (B) A book about saving money.

   (C) A job advertisement in the newspaper.

   (D) A booklet on different banking services.

2. The purpose of mentioning different countries and their tipping practices is _____ .

   (A) to show how knowledgeable the author is

   (B) to encourage people to stay in Taiwan

   (C) to warn people not to make mistakes when choosing a job

   (D) to point out that tipping culture is different from country to country

3. The word "**boorish**" in the third paragraph may be similar to _____ .

   (A) generous　　(B) satisfied　　(C) local　　(D) rude

4. The passage suggests readers to _____ before visiting a foreign country.

   (A) do a bit of research on the tipping culture

   (B) practice buying the waiter a drink

   (C) ask someone to travel with you

   (D) read more books about local food

5. Which of the following about tipping is **NOT** true?

   (A) Tipping is a way to show gratitude for the service.

   (B) French people always use the tips to buy themselves a drink.

   (C) People in Italy would leave small tips when they can afford them.

   (D) It is normal for Americans to tip people who serve them.

What is tipping?

It is also called "gratuity." It is a common way to express your gratitude by leaving money for someone who has offered a service to you.

Taiwan—
Tipping is not customary.

France—
The word for tipping means "to have a drink" in French. So, it's a friendly way to buy your waiter a glass of wine for a job well done.

Some Tipping Cultures Around the World

Italy—
It's not mandatory, but people often leave small tips if they can afford them.

America—
The tipping capital of the world. People leave a tip if they receive any services.

Ⓐ Word Bank

1. all of a sudden *phr.* 突然間
2. gratuity [grə`tjuətɪ] *n.* [C] 小費
3. gratitude [`grætə,tjud] *n.* [U] 感謝
4. customary [`kʌstəm,ɛrɪ] *adj.*
   慣常的
5. bewildering [bɪ`wɪldərɪŋ] *adj.*
   令人困惑的
6. mandatory [`mændə,torɪ] *adj.*
   強制的
7. presumably [prɪ`zuməblɪ] *adv.*
   大概；可能
8. starting point *n.* [C] 起點

🖉 Practice　請將 Word Bank 中的單字填入空格，並依句意做出適當變化

1. Carl always gives me a hand. I am really thankful, but I don't know what to do to show my _____ .
2. In many Asian countries, it is _____ to give out envelopes that contain money during the New Year holidays.
3. Because of her excellent service, the waitress received lots of _____ from the customers.
4. The young lady gave me directions to the bus stop, but I found them very _____ .
5. In 1997, the government made it _____ to wear helmets when people ride motorcycles.

Unit 11 旅遊 Travel

 Answer Key　1. gratitude　2. customary　3. gratuities　4. bewildering　5. mandatory

Unit 12

Art
Basic Level

⑦ Pre-reading Questions

1. What are the important elements of dance?

2. Do you know any famous dancers or dance troupes?

3. Where can you probably enjoy a live dance performance?

🔠 Target Vocabulary

assistance *n.*
幫助

folk *adj.*
民俗的

senior *adj.*
年長的

stroller *n.*
幼兒推車

retro *adj.*
懷舊的

Dance Through the Ages

Date: Saturday, September 22, 2018
Time: 13:30 to 17:00 at Wilson Hall

Do you love dancing? If yes, *Dance Through the Ages* is a top-rated① show for you. This musical will show you the history of dance. In addition, you'll learn about popular dance movements around the world. Interested? Check the program② out!

Show Time	Era	Name of Program and Dance Style	Country of Origin
13:30–13:40	Intro		
13:40–14:20	Medieval Ages③	Express life's joy—European dance	Europe
14:20–15:00	Late 15th century	English folk culture—Morris④ dance	England
15:00–15:20	Break Time		
15:20–16:20	Late 1940s	A short talk with the Gods—Mambo	Cuba
16:20–16:50	Mid-60s to early 70s	Retro⑤ nightlife style—Disco	America
16:50–17:00	Closing		

Ticket Information

1. NT$1,500 per person. (Order online to get an extra 10% discount!)

2. Senior⑥ citizens aged 65 and over can get 20% off by presenting the ID card.

3. Children aged 7 and under accompanied by parents can watch the show for free.

4. Free parking space up to 50 acres⑦ is available.

5. Special offer for military personnel⑧, civil⑨ servants, and teachers, up to 30% off.

6. Special assistance⑩, like wheelchairs or strollers⑪, is available at the information desk.

_____ 1. Nathan plans to go to the show with his family. His parents are in their seventies. His wife works in the town office. His two kids, aged 5 and 9, are coming along as well. How much will the admission be?

(A) NT$6,000.　(B) NT$7,500.　(C) NT$6,450.　(D) NT$5,400.

_____ 2. Lucy is into English culture and dance. Which of the following dance styles will she be interested?

(A) Morris dance.　　　(B) Disco.

(C) Mambo.　　　(D) European dance.

Ⓐ Word Bank

1. top-rated [ˌtɑp`retɪd] *adj.*
   非常受歡迎的
2. program [`progræm] *n.* [C] 節目單
3. medieval [ˌmidɪ`ivl̩] *adj.* 中世紀的
4. folk [fok] *adj.* 民俗的
5. retro [`rɛtro] *adj.* 懷舊的
6. senior [`sinjɚ] *adj.* 年長的

7. acre [`ekɚ] *n.* [C] 英畝
8. personnel [ˌpɝsn̩`ɛl] *n.* [U]
   (公司、組織或軍隊的) 全體人員
9. civil [`sɪvl̩] *adj.* 文職的
10. assistance [ə`sɪstəns] *n.* [U] 幫助
11. stroller [`strolɚ] *n.* [C] 幼兒推車

✏ Practice　請將 Word Bank 中的單字填入空格，並依句意做出適當變化

1. It is said that the first show on the _____ is a remarkable dance performance. I can't wait to see it.
2. The president's new policy will have a great impact on all _____ servants.
3. The government offers loans to students who need financial _____.
4. This _____ castle not only looks beautiful but carries cultural significance.
5. That famous restaurant around the corner is _____. It is fully occupied on weekends all the time.

Unit 12

Art
Intermediate Level

⑦ Pre-reading Questions

1. What do you think of when it comes to performance art?

2. What are some of the well-known Broadway shows you know?

3. Do you know how Broadway became famous for theaters?

🗚 Target Vocabulary

midtown *n.*
市中心

notable *adj.*
引人注目的

unknown *adj.*
不知名的

dedicated *adj.*
盡心盡力的

production *n.*
藝術作品

📖 Reading

Broadway, located in midtown① Manhattan, houses the city's famous theaters. Broadway played a prominent② role in the late 1800s and early 1900s, as theater owners moved there looking for places that were less expensive than other districts③ of the city. Nowadays, Broadway is an interesting and busy area, with lots of signs, people, lights, and actions. There are dozens of theaters in Broadway, with some being large and well-known, and the others small and relatively unknown④.

One of the largest and most notable⑤ theaters is the Majestic, which puts on huge musical theater productions⑥ like *Camelot* and *The Phantom of the Opera*, the longest-running show in the history of Broadway. Housing famous shows has established the Majestic as a great place to watch a show.

As an audience, you may be surprised by how much effort is put in to present a wonderful show. Performers on the stage are definitely the stars, but those who work behind the scenes, such as make-up artists, set designers, builders, producers, directors, and other professionals, are indispensable⑦ parts to the success of a show. Thanks to these people, we have incredible hits like *Chicago*, *Cats*, and *Les Misérables*, which together have put on more than 25,000 performances so far.

Next time when you have a chance to visit Broadway, don't just be a tourist taking pictures with the scenes and signs. Get a seat and watch a show. It will not only be a memorable⑧ experience, but also a real support for people dedicated⑨ to theaters.

_____ 1. What can be the best title for this passage?

    (A) The Production of the Broadway Show

    (B) How to Become Famous in Broadway

    (C) The Tourist's Guide in New York

    (D) Broadway: the Capital of Theater

_____ 2. Broadway gets its name for being _____.

(A) a less expensive area in New York

(B) home to many musical composers

(C) a famous place for theatergoers

(D) an area with lots of attractive signs

_____ 3. Which of the following is **NOT** mentioned in the passage for making a successful show?

(A) Actors.   (B) Make-up artists.

(C) Directors.   (D) Budget.

 **After You Read**

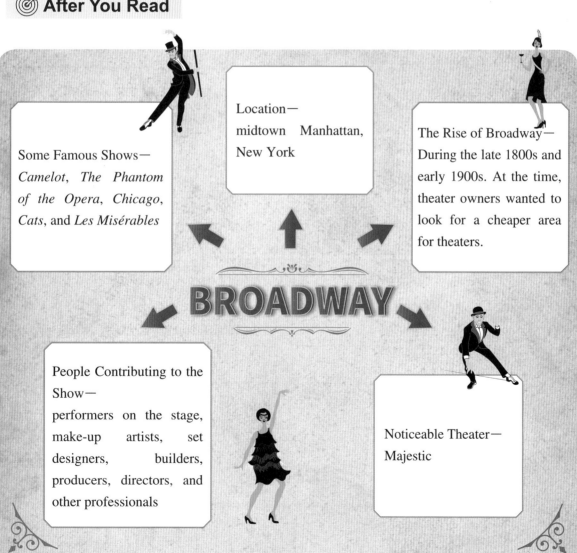

Some Famous Shows—
Camelot, *The Phantom of the Opera*, *Chicago*, *Cats*, and *Les Misérables*

Location—
midtown Manhattan, New York

The Rise of Broadway—
During the late 1800s and early 1900s. At the time, theater owners wanted to look for a cheaper area for theaters.

BROADWAY

People Contributing to the Show—
performers on the stage, make-up artists, set designers, builders, producers, directors, and other professionals

Noticeable Theater—
Majestic

Word Bank

1. midtown [ˋmɪdtaʊn] *n.* [U] 市中心
2. prominent [ˋprɑmənənt] *adj.*
   著名的
3. district [ˋdɪstrɪkt] *n.* [C] 區
4. unknown [ʌnˋnon] *adj.* 不知名的
5. notable [ˋnotəbl̩] *adj.* 引人注目的
6. production [prəˋdʌkʃən] *n.* [C]
   藝術作品

7. indispensable [͵ɪndɪˋspɛnsəbl̩]
   adj. 不可或缺的
8. memorable [ˋmɛmərəbl̩] *adj.*
   難忘的
9. dedicated [ˋdɛdə͵ketɪd] *adj.*
   盡心盡力的

✐ **Practice**   請將 Word Bank 中的單字填入空格，並依句意做出適當變化

1. To be a good kindergarten teacher, patience is a(n) _____ quality.
2. Ang Lee is a(n) _____ director, who is the first Asian person to win the Academy Award for Best Director twice.
3. Mr. Wang chose to live in the rural _____ in pursuit of a more relaxed lifestyle.
4. The price of milk has been going up because a(n) _____ disease caused a drop in the milk yield.
5. The legendary singer was given a lifetime achievement award in honor of his _____ contribution to music.

⑦ Pre-reading Questions

1. What do you usually do when you feel stressed?

2. Have you ever heard of Zentangle? What is it?

3. Why is Zentangle getting popular nowadays?

🔠 Target Vocabulary

goal-oriented *adj.*
目標導向的

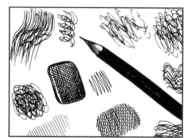

doodle *n.*
隨手亂畫

technical pen *n.*
針筆

clinical *adj.*
臨床的

meditation *n.*
冥想

📖 Reading

Zentangle is a way to create beautiful designs by drawing structured[1] patterns. The results may look like our doodles[2] in textbooks, but in fact, Zentangle involves a theory and a definite process. Rick Roberts and Maria Thomas originated the trademark[3] of the Zentangle theory and method.

Basically, it's a way of sketching images by using a technical pen[4] on a piece of white paper. Today, it is getting popular around the world and widely used in classrooms, clinical[5] psychology, art therapy[6], and meditation[7].

Although the Zentangle images seem sophisticated, they are simply the composition[8] of dots and lines. People of all ages can learn Zentangle from books or the Internet. For people who meditate, creating a Zentangle drawing makes them feel relaxed and focused. Moreover, experts say that Zentangle is healing because anyone can do it without any expectation and pressure. You just play with the pen, accepting the images that appear without any thoughts. Also, you learn to adapt the mistakes and change the images during the process. This is a life skill of making the best of our mistakes.

After mastering the skills of Zentangle, you can do it at will. This activity encourages people to be less goal-oriented[9] and less competitive. It teaches people to live in the moment. By enjoying the creative process, you begin to appreciate every single moment of it and relish[10] the process of personal creativity. Zentangle teaches people, "Don't rush. Pause to appreciate the present moment." No wonder more and more people indulge[11] themselves in the world of Zentangle.

_____ 1. What is Zentangle?

(A) It's a kind of doodle in textbooks.

(B) It's a pet owned by Rick and Maria.

(C) It's a way to draw by using dots and lines.

(D) It's a treatment widely used in the hospital.

_____ 2. How can people learn Zentangle?

(A) They naturally learn it when they turn 18.

(B) They can pick the skills up from books.

(C) They can learn it by meditating.

(D) They need to do it with the help of their doctors.

_____ 3. Which of the following is the feature of Zentangle?

(A) It is one way to relieve stress.

(B) Making mistakes is acceptable.

(C) It is formed by dots and lines.

(D) All of the above.

_____ 4. According to the passage, Zentangle is a nice way to relieve pressure. Who could be benefited most from it?

(A)

Anna

(B)

Master Sifu

(C)

Christopher

(D)

Linda

_____ 5. Which of the following is **NOT** the benefit people obtain from Zentangle?

(A) Being able to reach one's goal faster.

(B) Being able to enjoy living at the moment.

(C) Being capable of calming the restless mind.

(D) Being capable of accepting mistakes.

After You Read

What is Zentangle?	· It is a way of sketching images by using a technical pen on a piece of white paper. · The basic elements of a Zentangle image are dots and lines.
Who are the founders of Zentangle?	· Rick Roberts and Maria Thomas
Where can you find Zentangle?	· Zentangle is used in classrooms, clinical psychology, art therapy, meditation and more.
Who can do Zentangle?	· People of all ages can learn Zentangle.
What are some benefits that Zentangle brings about?	· Zentangle makes people feel relaxed and focused. · Zentangle has a healing effect. · Zentangle makes people accept making mistakes. By adapting a mistake, a new image will naturally appear.
What is the philosophy behind Zentangle?	· To live in the moment—"Don't rush. Pause to appreciate the present moment."

1. structured [`strʌktʃɚd] *adj.* 有組織的
2. doodle [`dudl̩] *n.* [C] 隨手亂畫
3. trademark [`tred,mɑrk] *n.* [C] 商標
4. technical pen *n.* [C] 針筆
5. clinical [`klınıkl̩] *adj.* 臨床的
6. therapy [`θɛrəpɪ] *n.* [U][C] 療法
7. meditation [,mɛdə`teʃən] *n.* [U] 冥想
8. composition [,kɑmpə`zıʃən] *n.* [U][C] 構圖；構成
9. goal-oriented [`gol `orı,ɛntɪd] *adj.* 目標導向的
10. relish [`rɛlıʃ] *vt.* 享受
11. indulge [ın`dʌldʒ] *vt.; vi.* 沉溺

✎ **Practice** 請將 Word Bank 中的單字填入空格，並依句意做出適當變化

1. Mrs. Yang has joined a yoga club. She practices breathing, stretching, and _____ there.

2. Nike's famous "Swoosh" symbol is a(n) _____ that is recognized worldwide.

3. Stop complaining! You should learn to appreciate and _____ the wonderful things in life.

4. Retirement allows Mr. Thomas to _____ himself in his passion for art. Now he has plenty of time to create artwork.

5. Our current situation made us realize that we need a more _____ approach to deal with the financial problem.

Unit 12 藝術 Art

Unit 13

Career
Basic Level

❓ **Pre-reading Questions**

1. What would you do if you were not satisfied with the product you ordered, or the service you received?

2. If you were a boss, what would you do when you received a complaint from your customers?

🔤 **Target Vocabulary**

blurred *adj.*
模糊的

refund *n.*
退款

lens *n.*
鏡頭

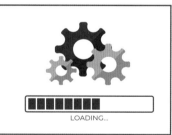

upgrade *vt.*
升級

heartfelt *adj.*
誠摯的

 **Reading**

From: Lauren Smith <lauren.smith@gmail.com>

To: Snappy Photos <contact@snappyphotos.com>

CC[①]: Oscar Halper <oscar.h2018@gmail.com>; Paul Smith <paulsmith8811@ttcompany.com>

Subject: Wedding Photos

July 24, 2018　13:28

Dear Snappy Photos,

　　I have received the video and photographs of my wedding. However, I am not pleased. Many of the photos were blurred[②] or overexposed[③]. I think the photographer should either upgrade[④] his camera or buy some new lenses[⑤].

　　The video was slightly better. However, the cameraman[⑥] didn't follow our instructions[⑦]. We were hoping that our guests could say a few words to the camera about my special day, but the cameraman only did this for two of the ten tables.

　　I think Snappy Photos should do something to make it up. I feel that I deserve a heartfelt[⑧] apology and some money back. Maybe not a full refund[⑨], but at least something that shows your company is taking responsibility for these mistakes.

Sincerely,

Lauren Smith

_____ 1. What is the main reason for Lauren to write this email?

(A) To express her happiness as a bride.

(B) To ask questions about her wedding photos.

(C) To blame the photographer for his bad attitude.

(D) To make a complaint about poor service.

　　　　　　2. What should the owner of Snappy Photos do based on the email?

　　　　　(A) Return the video and photos.

　　　　　(B) Offer another service for free.

　　　　　(C) Apologize and give a reasonable refund.

　　　　　(D) Make adjustments to the video and photos.

Ⓐ Word Bank

1. CC (= carbon copy) *abbr.* 副本
2. blurred [blɝd] *adj.* 模糊的
3. overexpose [`ovərɪk`spoz] *vt.* 使……過度曝光
4. upgrade [`ʌp`gred] *vt.* 升級
5. lens [lɛnz] *n.* [C] 鏡頭
6. cameraman [`kæmərə͵mæn] *n.* [C] 攝影師
7. instruction [ɪn`strʌkʃən] *n.* [C] 指示
8. heartfelt [`hɑrt͵fɛlt] *adj.* 誠摯的
9. refund [`ri͵fʌnd] *n.* [C] 退款

✐ Practice　請將 Word Bank 中的單字填入空格，並依句意做出適當變化

1. I need to _____ my operating system to the latest one before running this software.
2. Jason took the _____ off his camera after he got some good shots.
3. My glasses were _____ because of the steam from the hot tea.
4. I'm sorry for what I've done. Please accept my _____ apology.
5. If you don't like what you've purchased, you can return the item to the store with the receipt for a full _____.

⑦ Pre-reading Questions

1. Do you agree that gender affects how much one gets paid?

2. Why does the gender wage gap still exist in some countries?

3. Have you ever heard about some examples of the gender wage gap?

🔤 Target Vocabulary

salary *n.*
薪資

parity *n.*
平等

gap *n.*
差距

workplace *n.*
工作場所

gender *n.*
性別

 **Reading**

Beth and Charles are managers who work for the same company. They have the same job title and similar work experience. Most people who work with them would agree they bring equal value to the company. However, Beth's salary① is 20% less. This is due to the gender② wage③ gap④ in the workplace⑤.

The gender wage gap is a hidden rule of paying men higher salaries than women. Although many companies claim they don't do this, the stats suggest otherwise. Research indicates that women who work full-time earn about 20% less than men. Some claim this is because men and women choose different professions⑥. Yet, the gender wage gap still exists with people in the same profession. For example, in the US, over 70% of the teachers are female, but the average salary for male teachers is about 13% higher. The same principle applies to salespeople, lawyers, and several other fields.

In 2009, then US President Obama signed the Lilly Ledbetter Fair Pay Act. Nevertheless, many women still feel that **it** isn't changing fast enough. Women still get paid less than men at present. In fact, at the current⑦ pace of progress, some experts predict that it might take up to 98 years to reach "pay parity⑧." Hopefully⑨, the society can find some ways to eliminate⑩ gender discrimination⑪ and pay women what they truly deserve.

_____ 1. What is the gender wage gap?

    (A) It is a good way for companies to make a profit.

    (B) It is a stereotype of men and women in the society.

    (C) It is a common business practice when the economy is unstable.

    (D) It is a situation where men and women don't get equal pay for work of equal value.

_____ 2. What does the word "**it**" in the last paragraph refer to?

    (A) Gender stereotype.

    (B) Equal pay for work of equal value.

    (C) Work experience.

(D) The Lilly Ledbetter Fair Pay Act.

_____ 3. Which of the following is true about the passage?

(A) The gender wage gap only exists in few professions.

(B) In the US, 70% of the female teachers get paid more than their male colleagues.

(C) The gender wage gap will surely take place in 98 years.

(D) The gender wage gap needs to be closed in order to reach pay parity.

🎯 After You Read

· Introduction—The Gender Wage Gap Exists

Beth and Charles make the same contribution to their company; however, Beth's salary is 20% less. This is due to the gender wage gap in the workplace.

· Body—The Gender Wage Gap Is a Hidden Rule in Business Practices

· Reality check 1: As full-time workers, women get paid 20% less than men.

· Reality check 2: Teachers, salespeople, and lawyers are some examples of men and women doing the same job but being paid differently.

· Conclusion—Measures Need to Be Taken to Close the Gender Wage Gap

A Word Bank

1. salary [`sælərɪ] *n.* [U][C] 薪資
2. gender [`dʒɛndɚ] *n.* [U] 性別
3. wage [wedʒ] *n.* [C] 工資
4. gap [gæp] *n.* [C] 差距
5. workplace [`wɝk,ples] *n.* [C] 工作場所
6. profession [prə`fɛʃən] *n.* [C] 職業
7. current [`kɝənt] *adj.* 當前的
8. parity [`pærətɪ] *n.* [U] 平等；同等
9. hopefully [`hopfəlɪ] *adv.* 但願
10. eliminate [ɪ`lɪmə,net] *vt.* 消除
11. discrimination [dɪ,skrɪmə`neʃən] *n.* [U] 歧視

✏ Practice　請將 Word Bank 中的單字填入空格，並依句意做出適當變化

1. Black people in America used to live under the shadow of racial _____.
2. The female employees in that company are fighting for equal treatment in the _____.
3. If you want to keep your weight off, you should _____ fatty foods from your diet.
4. When asked about the _____ state of his company, the boss let out a deep sigh, telling me how much difficulty and pressure he had faced.
5. _____, we will have a bumper harvest of strawberries this winter.

Answer Key　1. discrimination　2. workplace　3. eliminate　4. current　5. Hopefully

Unit 13

Career
Advanced Level

⑦ Pre-reading Questions

1. Have you heard of the shokunin spirit?

2. Where does the term "shokunin spirit" come from and what does it represent?

3. Why is it important to have the shokunin spirit?

🔠 Target Vocabulary

routine *adj.*
例行公事的

vision *n.*
眼光

craftsman *n.*
工匠

raw *adj.*
生的

superior *adj.*
優越的

📖 Reading

Behind the counter of a small sushi restaurant in Tokyo, a master chef is at work. He carefully shapes every slice of raw[①] fish over sushi rice. Although he has been doing this for over 50 years, he believes he still has room for improvement. This is the spirit of "shokunin."

The concept of "shokunin" is an important part of Japanese culture. Although it's often defined[②] as a master craftsman[③], this literal description cannot precisely express its deeper meaning. In addition to superior[④] technique, a shokunin's obligation[⑤] is to care deeply about society and the people they serve. Perfection[⑥] may not exist, but a shokunin should remain focused and progress day by day.

No matter what career you have chosen, the principles behind the shokunin spirit can help you stay positive and work efficiently[⑦]. Here are a few tips to keep in mind. Try to begin the day with a clean working environment. An organized workspace can help sharpen your focus and boost your creativity. Next, cultivate[⑧] a positive attitude. Always take your work seriously, even if it seems boring. When you're repeating a simple task, try to do it with complete focus. Throughout the day, try to think of ways to improve your routine[⑨] work. Over time, these tiny improvements can add up and make the quality of your work better. Also, don't be afraid to be a bit stubborn[⑩]. Although a shokunin should be willing to listen to other people's opinions, they should trust their own vision[⑪].

The last and most important quality of the shokunin spirit is passion. In order to succeed at the highest level, you have to love what you're doing. In the world of a shokunin, it's impossible to create great art without dedication.

1. The term "shokunin" originated in _____.

(A) South Korea (B) Germany (C) Japan (D) Australia

2. A shokunin has the following beliefs EXCEPT that _____.

(A) there is always room for improvement

(B) it is necessary to do the same thing for 50 years

(C) being focused is the key to excellent quality

(D) it is important to have a passion for his or her career

3. Which of the following words is **NOT** suitable to describe a shokunin?

(A) Hard-working.   (B) Focused.

(C) Stubborn.   (D) Bored.

4. Where could you possibly see this passage?

(A) A career guide.   (B) A fashion magazine.

(C) A science journal.   (D) A government booklet.

5. Which of the following mottos does **NOT** match the shokunin spirit?

(A)

Continuously learn from nature.

(B)

Function and comfort are my lifelong pursuit.

(C)

The number of sales matters most. Show me the money!

(D)

Customers' satisfaction is my ultimate goal.

An Interview with a Shokunin

 Where are you from?

I am from Japan.

 What do you do? And how long have you been doing this?

I am a sushi master, and I've been doing this for 50 years.

 Do you consider yourself a shokunin?

Yes, but I am just trying my best to satisfy my customers.

 In your opinion, what is the key to be a shokunin?

First, constant improvement. Then, focus on your work and be happy to serve. Third, have your own idea, and it's OK to be a little bit stubborn. Last but not least, always have passion for what you do.

A Word Bank

1. raw [rɔ] *adj.* 生的
2. define [dɪ`faɪn] *vt.* 給……下定義
3. craftsman [`kræftsmən] *n.* [C] 工匠
4. superior [sə`pɪrɪɚ] *adj.* 優越的
5. obligation [ˌɑblə`geʃən] *n.* [C][U] 義務;職責
6. perfection [pɚ`fɛkʃən] *n.* [U] 完美
7. efficiently [ɪ`fɪʃəntlɪ] *adv.* 高效率地
8. cultivate [`kʌltə‚vet] *vt.* 養成
9. routine [ru`tin] *adj.* 例行公事的
10. stubborn [`stʌbɚn] *adj.* 頑固的
11. vision [`vɪʒən] *n.* [U] 眼光

Practice 請將 Word Bank 中的單字填入空格,並依句意做出適當變化

1. Jerry has made plans for his next ten years. I think he is a man of great _____.

2. In certain countries, male citizens above 18 have the _____ to serve in the army.

3. Mr. Brown is as _____ as a mule. He never listens to others.

4. The ability to appreciate art can be _____ through some related courses or visits to museums.

5. Sally's _____ skills in English made her qualified for the job.

Unit 13 職場 Career

Unit 14

Disaster Prevention
Basic Level

⑦ Pre-reading Questions

1. What is a natural disaster?
2. When you read the news about natural disasters, what information would you pay attention to?

🔠 Target Vocabulary

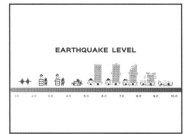

magnitude *n.*
震度

donation *n.*
捐獻

homeless *n.*
無家可歸者

tropical *adj.*
熱帶的

rainfall *n.*
降雨量

 **Reading**

A severe① earthquake hit 816 Island shortly after 8:00 a.m. last Friday. To make matters worse, a tropical② storm struck the island in the afternoon. The storm brought 75 mph③ winds and 20 mm of rainfall④ in 10 hours. Early reports showed that lots of people were injured and even killed. In addition, thousands of people have lost their homes. Experts believe the disaster has caused more than 13 billion⑤ dollars in damages. Several nations are offering their support. For example, the United States and France have sent medical teams, daily necessities, and nearly $10 million dollars in the form of humanitarian⑥ aid.

Earthquake Information

Location: 816 Island

Time & Date: 8:03 a.m., 8/16/2018

Magnitude⑦: 6.4

Injured	324
Dead	53
Homeless⑧	7,000 (estimated)
Economic Damages	$13 billion in damage (estimated)
Donation⑨	$10 million (total so far)

_____ 1. From the report, how many people were injured in the disaster?

(A) 53.   (B) 700.   (C) 324.   (D) 75.

_____ 2. According to the report, which of the following support was **NOT** offered by foreign countries?

(A) Community recovery.   (B) Medical team.

(C) Donation.   (D) Daily necessities.

Ⓐ Word Bank

1. severe [sə`vɪr] *adj.* 慘重的
2. tropical [`trɑpɪkl] *adj.* 熱帶的
3. mph (=miles per hour) *abbr.* 每小時行駛英里數
4. rainfall [`ren,fɔl] *n.* [U] 降雨量
5. billion [`bɪljən] *n.* [C] 十億
6. humanitarian [hju,mænə`tɛrɪən] *adj.* 人道主義的
7. magnitude [`mægnə,tjud] *n.* [C] 震度
8. homeless [`homləs] *n.* [plural] 無家可歸者
9. donation [do`neʃən] *n.* [C][U] 捐獻

✎ Practice 　請將 Word Bank 中的單字填入空格，並依句意做出適當變化

1. With generous _____ from several companies, the hospital was built under budget, and the remaining money was used to buy medical equipment.

2. With proper care and treatment, the little girl made a good recovery from the _____ car accident.

3. The Sahara is the largest desert in the world, and its average _____ is less than 100 mm each year.

4. Jason was amazed by the snow because he grew up in a _____ country where it never snows.

5. According to the scientists, the earth came into existence _____ of years ago.

⑦ Pre-reading Questions

1. How many nuclear power plants are there in Taiwan? Where are they located?
2. How much do you know about nuclear power?
3. What are other types of energy people can use besides nuclear power?

🄰 Target Vocabulary

protester *n.*
抗議者

sediment *n.*
沉澱物

opt *vi.*
選擇

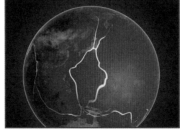

fault line *n.*
斷層線

debris *n.*
碎片

🎒 Reading

In 2011, a disaster in Japan sent shock waves around the world. The massive earthquake along with the subsequent① nuclear② crisis has not only caused problems in Japan but also raised concerns in other countries. Taiwan, the island situated on earthquake fault lines③, should learn lessons from Japan and rethink the future of nuclear power.

Not having the advantage of fossil fuel④ reserves, Taiwan has opted⑤ for nuclear power for decades. Currently, Taiwan has three active nuclear power plants with six reactors⑥. All of them are run by the Taiwan Power Company (Taipower). According to the statistics, nuclear power makes up almost 10 percent of Taiwan's national energy consumption⑦. Now, the crisis in Japan at the Fukushima Daiichi Nuclear Power Plant is causing many to doubt how safe Taiwan's nuclear power plants are.

Some reports indicate that there may exist unsafe conditions at the Kuosheng Nuclear Power Plant in Wanli, New Taipei City. To be more specific, the plant's suppression pools⑧ are said to have contained high amounts of sediment⑨, debris⑩, and waste materials, which could be dangerous in the case of a nuclear emergency. A spokesperson⑪ for Taipower states that these areas have been cleaned and the Kuosheng plant has also been scheduled for regular cleaning. Moreover, some have pointed out that Taiwan's nuclear power plants use boiling water reactors, which are similar to the reactors found at the Fukushima Daiichi plant in Japan.

Anti-nuclear protesters⑫ gathered on Ketagalan Boulevard after the disaster happened in Japan. They appealed to the government with the slogan "No nukes⑬, No more Fukushima." It's going to be a challenge for the government to strike a balance between energy demand and the environment.

_____ 1. According to the passage, how many active nuclear power plants are there in Taiwan?

(A) 6.　　　　　(B) 3.　　　　　(C) 10.　　　　　(D) 2.

2. People express concerns over the nuclear power plants in Taiwan because the reactors are _____.

    (A) bought from Japan

    (B) the main cause of noise pollution

    (C) similar to the ones found in Fukushima

    (D) not efficient and need regular cleaning

3. If there is a sequel to this passage, what will be a suitable topic to be discussed?

    (A) The budget for the fourth nuclear power plant in Taiwan.

    (B) An alternative to nuclear power.

    (C) How to organize an anti-nuclear protesters.

    (D) How nuclear disaster made Taiwan and Japan closer.

◎ After You Read

Introduction

The nuclear disaster in Japan in 2011 raised people's concerns over the nuclear safety.

Body

1. Taiwan relies on nuclear power because it does not have natural fossil fuel reserves. Therefore, nuclear power plays an important role in Taiwan's national energy consumption.

2. Taiwanese have safety concerns about nuclear power plants since Taiwan uses similar reactors to the ones in Japan. Also, there seems to be negligence on the maintenance of these nuclear power plants.

Conclusion

The appeal made by anti-nuclear protestants poses further challenges for the government in future nuclear power development.

Unit 14 防災 Disaster Prevention

Ⓐ Word Bank

1. subsequent [ˈsʌbsɪ,kwənt] *adj.* 接著的
2. nuclear [ˈnjuklɪɚ] *adj.* 核能的
3. fault line *n.* [C] 斷層線
4. fossil fuel *n.* [U] 礦物燃料
5. opt [ɑpt] *vi.* 選擇
6. reactor [rɪˈæktɚ] *n.* [C] 核反應堆
7. consumption [kənˈsʌmpʃən] *n.* [U] 消耗量
8. suppression pool *n.* [C] 抑壓池
9. sediment [ˈsɛdəmənt] *n.* [U] 沉澱物
10. debris [dəˈbrɪ] *n.* [U] 碎片
11. spokesperson [ˈspoks,pɝsṇ] *n.* [C] 發言人
12. protester [prəˈtɛstɚ] *n.* [C] 抗議者
13. nuke [njuk] *n.* [C] 核武器

✎ Practice 請將 Word Bank 中的單字填入空格，並依句意做出適當變化

1. The Industrial Revolution is indeed a milestone in human history. It has led to the _____ technological advancement

2. To lower power _____, Andy managed to cut down the time he used household appliances.

3. Though the police tried to communicate with the _____, they refused to leave.

4. The _____ for the victims' families criticized the airline for not taking full responsibility for the air crash.

5. The residents organized a march against the construction project of a new _____ power plant in the nearby area.

ⓘ Pre-reading Questions

1. What are some natural disasters that often hit Taiwan?

2. What are some ways to help people better cope with natural disasters?

🔤 Target Vocabulary

thunderstorm *n.*
雷雨

survival kit *n.*
急救箱

unpredictable *adj.*
無法預測的

tsunami *n.*
海嘯

tornado *n.*
龍捲風

🛢 Reading

Earthquakes, tornadoes①, tsunamis②, volcanoes, and typhoons—what do these natural disasters have in common? They are all unpredictable③ but inevitable④. That's why people feel worried or scared in the face of natural disasters. In Taiwan, the two main threats are earthquakes and typhoons. Both are powerful enough to destroy everything. The aftermath⑤ like landslide⑥ or flooding could damage houses and leave people homeless. However, with some preparation and knowledge in mind, we can react faster and better when natural disasters take place.

Here are some tips to follow. When it comes to typhoons, staying indoors would be the best choice. Make sure you have enough water and food at home. Check your surrounding area up and down to make sure that it won't flood when thunderstorms⑦ ensue⑧. Additionally, since the power may be cut off, you need to prepare flashlights and backup batteries⑨ just in case. As for earthquakes, it is necessary to practice earthquake drills regularly because there is no warning before an earthquake strikes. Make sure you know the evacuation⑩ routes⑪ and keep them clear all the time. Having a survival kit⑫ handy is a smart choice. When the earthquake is getting out of control, you may consider leaving the building as quickly as possible.

Natural disasters might be unavoidable, but by planning ahead, we can give ourselves a better chance to survive. As the saying goes, "**an ounce⑬ of prevention is worth a pound of cure.**" It won't hurt to get ready for natural disasters.

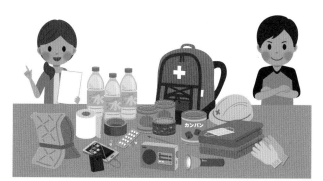

_____ 1. What is the purpose of this passage?

   (A) To categorize different types of natural disasters.

   (B) To exaggerate the damage caused by natural disasters.

   (C) To offer tips on how to react in the face of natural disasters.

   (D) To inform readers of the danger of typhoons and earthquakes.

_____ 2. According to the passage, which of the following natural disasters often hit Taiwan?

   (A) Tsunamis and earthquakes.

   (B) Earthquakes and typhoons.

   (C) Typhoons and volcano eruptions.

   (D) Tornadoes and tsunamis.

_____ 3. Why are people afraid of natural disasters?

   (A) Natural disasters are not powerful.

   (B) Natural disasters are inevitable.

   (C) Natural disasters are predictable.

   (D) Natural disasters are not common.

_____ 4. According to the passage, people should **NOT** _____ when a typhoon strikes.

   (A) leave the house immediately

   (B) stay away from the flooding zone

   (C) have plenty of backup electricity

   (D) prepare enough food and water

_____ 5. Which of the following is similar to "**an ounce of prevention is worth a pound of cure**" in the last paragraph?

   (A) Time and tide wait for no man.

   (B) An apple a day keeps the doctor away.

   (C) One skill is better than a million dollars.

   (D) Some people walk in the rain, others just get wet.

🎯 After You Read

Introduction

Natural disasters are unpredictable and inevitable.

Typhoons and earthquakes are two major natural disasters in Taiwan.

How to prepare for typhoons:
- ☺ stay indoors
- ☺ stock enough food and water
- ☺ check potential flooding areas
- ☺ have backup electricity

How to react to earthquakes:
- ☺ practice earthquake drills regularly
- ☺ know your evacuation route
- ☺ have a survival kit around
- ☺ leave the building if the earthquake is getting strong

Conclusion

"An ounce of prevention is worth a pound of cure." It won't hurt to get ready for natural disasters.

A Word Bank

1. tornado [tɔr`nedo] *n.* [C] 龍捲風
2. tsunami [tsu`nɑmɪ] *n.* [C] 海嘯
3. unpredictable [ˌʌnprɪ`dɪktəbḷ] *adj.* 無法預測的
4. inevitable [ɪn`ɛvətəbḷ] *adj.* 不可避免的
5. aftermath [`æftɚˌmæθ] *n.* [C] (不愉快事件的) 後果
6. landslide [`lændˌslaɪd] *n.* [C] 山崩
7. thunderstorm [`θʌndɚˌstɔrm] *n.* [C] 雷雨
8. ensue [ɛn`su] *vi.* 接著發生
9. battery [`bætərɪ] *n.* [C] 電池
10. evacuation [ɪˌvækju`eʃən] *n.* [C] 疏散
11. route [rut] *n.* [C] 路線
12. survival kit *n.* [C] 急救箱
13. ounce [auns] *n.* [C] 少量；少許

✎ Practice　請將 Word Bank 中的單字填入空格，並依句意做出適當變化

1. With the closure of the factory, it was _____ that many employees ended up being out of work.
2. There's not a(n) _____ of usefulness of Steve's project. No wonder his manager decided to cancel the meeting immediately.
3. Most hikers take this _____ to the mountain top in order to enjoy the view on the way.
4. It was a tragedy that the whole village was destroyed by a massive _____ following the earthquake.
5. As soon as the forest fire broke out, the government immediately arranged for the emergency _____ of local residents.

Unit 14 防災 Disaster Prevention

20分鐘稱霸統測英文對話

劉妃欽、莊靜軒／編著

- 十五回單元設計，完整收錄近年共60個統測對話必考情境。
- 獨家主題式情境對話編寫，並搭配跨頁圖解實用句，使讀者身歷其境，學習效果加倍。
- 版面編排活潑，配合中文翻譯，方便讀者完整對照。
- 豐富的小知識補充及英語加油站，增進知識、提升英語能力，完整瞄準統測對話延伸學習。
- 全新撰寫的單元試題，可測驗對話熟悉度，並附歷屆試題，有助掌握統測出題脈絡。
- 獨家附贈對話手冊，完整蒐集日常生活及統測實用問答句，重點迅速複習。

108課綱
贏戰統測

20分鐘
稱霸統測

英文
閱讀測驗

解析本

吳昱樺 編著

- 坊間唯一主打「素養導向」的統測閱讀測驗參考書
- 全書收錄 7 大閱讀解題技巧與精選 14 大閱測主題
- 訓練考生 20 分鐘完成統測閱讀測驗單元

東大圖書公司

Unit 1

Fashion 流行

初階 (Basic Level)

在 Pricee 進行網購

　　凱倫想買些禮物給她的家人，因為她剛收到績效獎金。由於凱倫的行程非常緊湊，她決定在非常受歡迎的線上購物網站 Pricee 採購。這些是她想看一下的。

爸爸

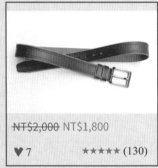
~~NT$2,000~~ NT$1,800
♥ 7　　★★★★★ (130)

約翰

~~NT$1,500~~ NT$1,200
♥ 20　　★★★★★ (150)

媽媽

~~NT$2,300~~ NT$1,900
♥ 13　　★★★★★ (367)

艾咪

~~NT$1,190~~ NT$1,150
♥ 7　　★★★★★ (175)

訂購與購物資訊

* 只有超過新臺幣 1,000 元的訂單可以免運。否則，需支付 60 元的運費。

* 快申辦你的 Pricee 會員卡！一年只需花費新臺幣 1,000 元。然而，每筆訂單都可以打九折。

* 在 Pricee，每買新臺幣 1,000 元可獲得紅利回饋點數 100 點。

　(詳情請見「紅利回饋方案」連結)

* 我們提供良好的售後服務。你買的任何東西 7 天內均可退貨並拿回退款。你只需支付運費。

特別聲明

* 任何一位買家的每筆訂單，滿新臺幣一萬元即可參加東京來回機票抽獎。

1

■ 正確解答 1.(C) 2.(B)

■ 難題解析

1. 文中提到 VIP 會員的話，每筆消費可打九折。因此，所有禮物的款項加總為新臺幣 6,050 元，打完折後為新臺幣 5,445 元，答案選 (C)。　*Making Inferences*

2. 文中提到，如需退換商品，需在購買 7 天內提出申請，答案選 (B)。　*Making Inferences*

中階 (Intermediate Level)

成為 YouTube 明星

　　成為全職 YouTuber 是許多年輕人的夢想工作。這讓你能隨心所欲地在任何地方工作，而且不必聽命於老闆。此外，你可以做真正喜愛的工作，還能收入優渥。如果這聽起來很吸引你，繼續讀下去！我將與你分享一些如何成為成功 YouTuber 的秘訣。

　　首先，在開始錄影片之前，為你的頻道選擇焦點是很重要的事。嘗試選擇一個你熱愛的主題，因為你將錄製數百支相關影片。你的頻道一旦啟動，定期製播新影片很重要。你該把目標放在每週至少出一支新影片。隨著你的頻道成長，你該開始接觸其他成功的 YouTuber，尋找合作機會。他們可以把你介紹給他們的訂戶，增加你的曝光率。最終，這會是雙贏局面，你倆都將贏得更多粉絲。

　　務必牢記，做頂尖的 YouTuber 需要耐性並勤奮工作。在開始吸引追蹤者之前，可能連續好幾個月都要拍片。誰知道呢？也許有天你會成為下一位網路超級巨星。

■ 正確解答 1.(D) 2.(D) 3.(C)

■ 難題解析

1. 此處的代名詞指的是前一句的主詞—成為全職 YouTuber 一事，答案選 (D)。
　　References

2. 第二段說明成為成功 YouTuber 的訣竅，當中提到選擇頻道焦點、定期製播新影片，以及和其他 YouTuber 合作創造更多曝光率，答案選 (D)。　*Supporting Details*

3. 本文第一段提及 YouTuber 是許多人的夢幻職業，故 (A) 有誤；第二段提到頻道焦點應該是以 YouTuber 自身熱愛的主題方向來經營，故 (B) 有誤；文章中並未提及錄製影片需要多久的時間，故 (D) 有誤；第二段倒數第三句提到與其他 YouTuber 合作是提升曝光率的方式，答案選 (C)。　*Making Inferences*

高階 (Advanced Level)

Netflix 的崛起

瑞德·海斯汀在 1997 年成立的 Netflix，是現今娛樂業最大媒體服務供應商。起初，在百視達還是當時業界的龍頭老大時，Netflix 透過郵寄租售 DVD。Netflix 希望提供更便利的服務，如此一來，顧客毋須離家就能租片來看。2007 年時，Netflix 發現商機，改變它的商業模式。<u>該公司決定利用網路轉變為串流媒體平臺</u>。這是個艱困的挑戰，但冒險最終獲得回報。百視達於 2010 年潰敗破產。

自 2018 年起，Netflix 擴張至全球。該公司現有逾 1 億訂戶，在大約 200 個國家營運。為了持續吸引新訂戶，Netflix 不斷努力改善服務。它甚至開始製作原創電視劇集，例如《怪奇物語》和《紙牌屋》，給會員帶來許多樂趣。

雖然 Netflix 是串流影音業霸主，但仍有不少競爭者。例如，Hulu 試圖提供用戶更便宜的月費方案以增加市占率。然而，它的片庫比 Netflix 小，且經濟型方案強迫用戶看廣告。另一個例子是 YouTube。它也推出串流服務，但有一些觀賞限制。Netflix 的最大威脅來自亞馬遜付費影音。它提供類似服務且持續擴張。為了保持領先地位，Netflix 必須努力產製優秀內容，以建立聲望。否則，它可能成為下一個百視達。

■ 正確解答 1.(C) 2.(A) 3.(C) 4.(B) 5.(B)

■ 難題解析

1. 本文主旨在介紹 Netflix 如何崛起以及未來可能面對的挑戰，答案選 (C)。　*Main Idea*

2. 由上下文可知，Netflix 的轉型是個不容易的挑戰，故選 (A)。　*Words in Context*

3. 由第二段可知，自 2018 年起，Netflix 在全球約 200 個國家營運，並有逾 1 億訂戶，故選 (C)。　*Supporting Details*

4. 由第三段第二句可知，Hulu 的價錢比 Netflix 便宜，故 (B) 不正確，答案選 (B)。
   Supporting Details

5. 第一段最後提到百視達被 Netflix 擊敗而退出市場，故 (A) 有誤；第二段最後提到，《紙牌屋》為 Netflix 的自製影集，故 (C) 有誤；第三段第四句提到，YouTube 有觀賞的限制，故 (D) 有誤；第三段倒數第三句提到，Amazon Prime Video 是 Netflix 的最大威脅，答案選 (B)。　*Supporting Details*

初階 (Basic Level)

全球各地的街頭食物

傑克・杜朗

　　杜朗是歐洲最炙手可熱的年輕主廚之一。他很小就發展出對廚藝的興趣。自巴黎料理名校藍帶廚藝學院畢業後，他在名廚艾曼紐・奧利佛手下工作了兩年。杜朗在休閒時，愛彈吉他和觀看電視上的足球賽。

泰勒・史密斯

　　過去 10 年，史密斯主要替《紐約時報》評鑑餐廳。她談美食時生花妙筆，在全球贏得成千上萬的粉絲。不僅是位食物評論家，她還是個語言天才，能說法、中、德、英四種語言。

克莉斯汀・李

　　李是評價很高的譯者。她能說流利的英語、法語、德語，和她的母語中文。有著絕佳的語言才能，她將一些經典名著譯成英文。她大多數的譯作都是亞馬遜網路書店的暢銷書。

■ 正確解答 1.(D) 2.(B)

■ 難題解析

1. 由文章中所搭配的圖可知，此書的作者為傑克・杜朗，答案選 (D)。　　*Supporting Details*

2. 由文章介紹到譯者，可推論此著作有被翻譯成英文，答案選 (B)。

　　Making Inferences

中階 (Intermediate Level)

和江振誠一起做料理

　　江振誠是臺灣的明星主廚。在他的職涯當中，這位 **42 歲主廚以其獨創的「八角哲學」料理風格，贏得不少獎項。**江振誠相信，每一餐都該具有 *八種關鍵元素，提供食客最大滿足。他不僅要求自己的料理要美味，也要帶來愉悅的回憶。

　　江振誠雖然在臺灣出生，但童年大多待在日本。最初，他被寄望繼承家業，但他對美食很有熱情，想成為一名廚師。為了圓夢，江振誠搬到法國，花了 15 年向國內頂尖主廚學習。這些珍貴經驗啟發他的想像力，激發他的創造力。2010 年，他在新加坡經營自己的餐廳 André，很快成為後起之秀。

　　2017 年，當江振誠宣布關掉他在新加坡著名的米其林二星餐廳 André 時，震撼了整個餐飲界。江振誠也歸還他贏得的米其林星星。這個決定讓他得以回臺灣開新餐廳 RAW。現在，他的主要重心是訓練臺灣年輕的廚師，也多了解他的家鄉文化。江振誠說：「我很高興也願意做一扇窗。那是我的優先要務。」

* 江振誠的八種元素是：鹽、質感、回憶、純淨、風土、南方、工匠和獨特。

■ 正確解答 1.(D) 2.(B) 3.(D)

■ 難題解析

1. 最後一段提到江振誠關閉新加坡餐廳最主要的原因是想回臺灣，一方面是傳承，另一方面則是尋根紮根，故選 (D)。　　*Supporting Details*

2. 第二段提到，江振誠花了 15 年在法國跟頂尖主廚學習廚藝，選項 (B) 敘述有誤，答案選 (B)。　　*Supporting Details*

3. 文章中提到的窗戶是一種比喻用法，江振誠希望自己在異地的經驗可以讓臺灣有志在餐飲界發光的後起之秀學習參考，故選 (D)。　　*Making Inferences*

高階 (Advanced Level)

史丹・李：超級英雄漫畫作者的一生

　　在漫畫世界，史丹・李是一個傳奇人物。他身為漫威漫畫的作者和編輯已超過 75 年。在這段職涯裡，他創造了許多知名的超級英雄，像是蜘蛛人、美國隊長和 X 戰警。

　　李早年的人生充滿挑戰。出生於二十世紀早期，經濟大蕭條期間，因此他了解到為生活掙扎是什麼樣子。李記得他的父母總是勉力維持生計。由於不願面對現實，李經常讓自己沉迷在電影和書籍中來藉此逃避。

　　1939 年，靠著叔叔的幫忙，他在漫威漫畫的前身「及時漫畫」找到一份工作。一開始，他大部分被指派的工作內容都很單調無聊，例如給鋼筆沾墨水和替同事訂午餐。然而，當兩名頂尖員工於 1941 年離職時，李有個機會鹹魚翻身。李接替他們的編輯和寫作職務。漸漸地，隨著作品的累積，他名揚全世界。

　　李創造超級英雄的其中一項特色，就是他們並非完美無瑕。例如，無敵的浩克力大無窮，卻不能控制他的脾氣。夜魔俠五種感官裡有四種比常人靈敏，卻雙目失明。史丹・李想讓虛幻人物變得「真實」。超級英雄仍有一些缺陷，就像你我一樣。

　　在 2018 年，史丹・李過世時享齡 95 歲。雖然李已不在我們的身邊，他傳奇的一生和作品仍常存。更甚者，他對漫畫的熱情感染了我們，使我們愛上他所創造的角色。

■ 正確解答 1.(A) 2.(C) 3.(A) 4.(A) 5.(D)

■ 難題解析

1. 文章中第一段第二句即可知道，史丹・李是漫威作者及編輯，答案選 (A)。
   Supporting Details

2. 由第二段的經濟大蕭條，以及李經常讓自己沉迷在電影、書籍，藉此逃避困苦的現實生活，推測李的家庭經濟狀況有困境，故答案選 (C)。　　*Words in Context*

3. 由上下文提及李的工作內容是給鋼筆沾墨水和替同事訂午餐，可推測 humdrum 與「無聊」最接近，答案選 (A)。　　*Words in Context*

4. 第四段提到李所創作的人物並非完美無瑕，好讓讀者能產生連結，答案選 (A)。
   Supporting Details

初階 (Basic Level)

傑瑞米的畢業派對

親愛的朋友，

　　為了慶祝我們畢業，我想要在下週六辦個派對。歡迎大家一起來玩！可以來的人，請在這個週末之前傳 LINE 訊息給我。

時間：2018 年 9 月 22 日，下午 3:00 到 9:30

地點：大佳河濱公園 6 號區

手機號碼：0912-321-321

活動：特製雞尾酒 (免費續杯)、精緻自助晚餐、專業現場樂隊演奏

傑瑞米　敬上

方向指引

搭捷運棕線往臺北南港展覽館方向，在大直站下車。從 1 號出口出站，轉乘 72 或 222 號公車，然後在「大佳國小」站下車。依照路標指示，約步行 7 至 10 分鐘，可到大佳河濱公園。

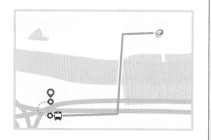

■ 正確解答 1.(A) 2.(C)

■ 難題解析

1. 由邀請函中的活動可知，並沒有煙火表演，答案選 (A)。　　*Supporting Details*

2. 根據傑瑞米所建議的交通方式，應為搭捷運 → 轉乘公車 → 步行至大佳河濱公園 6 號區，答案選 (C)。　　*Making Inferences*

中階 (Intermediate Level)

人工智慧：未來就在你的門前

　　想像行動雜貨店來到你家門前。你只需進入店裡，挑選你需要的品項，用你的智慧型手機掃描，然後離開。想像一下搭乘你永遠不必觸碰方向盤的自動駕駛汽車去旅行。想像孩童在學校由機器人授課。再想像一下登記入住旅館時可以不必排隊。你能想像這樣的生活嗎？

　　所有這些難以置信的構想，因為人工智慧而正逐漸成為事實。 人工智慧是一種讓電腦能像人類一樣思考的科學。人工智慧可追溯到 1955 年，因為速度及可以搜集和分析各式數據的因素而取得重要性。雖然我們對人工智慧的認識可能還不夠，但我們的房子、車子、銀行和手機都在使用它。它對我們的生活所產生的衝擊還在持續擴大。而且，人工智慧幾乎對我們生活的每一面向都有影響，例如教育、金融，甚至是健康照護。我們必須確保人工智慧應用在改善我們的生活方面，要不然它也許對我們有害。

- 正確解答 1.(C) 2.(D) 3.(A)
- 難題解析

1. 由第二段第二句對 AI 的定義解釋，可知人工智慧就是讓電腦可以像人類一樣思考的科學，故選 (C)。　*Main Idea*

2. 本篇文章的主題是科技，故可推論可能會在科技迷朋友的臉書貼文分享中看到這篇文章，故選 (D)。　*Making Inferences*

3. 文章中第一段所舉的例子並未提到下西洋棋的機器人，故選 (A)。　*Supporting Details*

高階 (Advanced Level)

無人機論戰：利弊分析

　　綜觀歷史，人們一直對飛行及飛行機具深感興趣。時至今日，這種入迷的表現，在無人機或正式稱為無人飛行載具上，仍持續發生。簡言之，無人機是一種遠端遙控的飛行器，也就是裡面沒有駕駛。而是由地面上的人，以手持控制器決定無人機往哪裡飛，以及做些什麼事。**由於無人機越來越受歡迎，被用來執行五花八門的任務，有關無人機的利弊得失便出現論戰。**

　　無人機的優點是，它有改變眾多產業運作方式的潛力。例如，亞馬遜之類的公司可以採用無人機取代貨車遞送包裹給顧客。這樣既省時間又省成本。同時，新聞業可以運用無人機去拍攝衝突區，這樣做不只減少風險，也能保護他們的記者和攝影師。最後，將無人機應用於軍事領域投入現代戰爭，能執行那些原先可能危及飛行員生命的危險任務。

另一方面，無人機也引起了一些擔憂。安全和隱私似乎是提到無人機的兩大顧慮。例如，由於人人都能購買和操作無人機，它們可能讓天空變得不安全。此外，無人機可以不引人注意地搜集影像，讓人們擔憂隱私遭受侵害。基於軍事理由，無人機能在哪裡以及怎麼飛，必須制定一些法規。它們應該被禁止進入管制區，例如軍用區域和訓練基地。

鑒於無人機產業發展快速，我們不可能因為少數缺點，便抗拒或忽視無人機在我們生活中的存在。只要我們善用無人機，仍能享受它們為生活所帶來的便利。

■ 正確解答 1.(C) 2.(D) 3.(B) 4.(A) 5.(C)

■ 難題解析

1. 文章第一段即介紹無人機的特徵，其中並未提到裡面沒有電池，故 (C) 有誤，答案選 (C)。 *Supporting Details*

2. 文章中第二段提到無人機的優點，但侵犯人們的隱私是無人機令人詬病的隱憂，故選 (D)。 *Supporting Details*

4. 文章中第三段提到無人機的缺點可知，無人機太容易取得可能讓天空變得不安全，答案選 (A)。 *Supporting Details*

5. 由文章中最後一段可知，作者認為只要我們善用無人機，便可享受它們所帶來的便利，因此作者的態度是支持的，答案選 (C)。 *Purpose and Tone*

Unit 4

Energy 能源

初階 (Basic Level)

逾期電費帳單

波士頓瓦斯電力公司
www.bostongasandelectric.com
美國麻州波士頓芬威路 162 號

2020 年 3 月 5 日

這項訊息是提醒您，積欠波士頓瓦斯電力公司的部分金額已逾截止期限。請立即繳款以免服務中斷。如果我們未在 30 天內收到款項，將被迫中斷您的電力供應。一旦斷電，您必須繳清全額，以及復電額外所需的 50 美元接通費。如果您有財務困難，請來電告知，我們可以協助您想出一個付款方案。您可以撥打 1-800-464-2729 聯絡我們的服務代表。

帳號	戶名	服務地址	費率
42729374937	寶琳‧華特生	美國麻州波士頓懷爾德巷 342 號	大型通用類

計費期間		帳單截止日	帳單類型	用量 (瓩)	逾期金額	帳單總金額
2020/01/01	2020/01/31	2020/02/28	010	126,470	$160.81	$227.04

2020 年 1 月帳單

電費	$43
瓦斯費	$6
州稅	$7.23
逾期費用	$10
總計：	**$66.23**

- 正確解答 1.(A) 2.(D)

- 難題解析

    1. 本通知主要在告知使用者帳單逾期未繳納，故選 (A)。 *Main Idea*

    2. 因已過了最後付款限期，所有帳款應為 $227.04 + $50 (線路接通費) = $277.04，故選 (D)。 *Supporting Details*

中階 (Intermediate Level)

- -

日光節約時間值得保留嗎？

　　每年春天，大約 **70** 個國家的人民會將他們的時鐘往前調快一個小時，開始「日光節約時間」**(DST)**，也稱作夏令時間。到了秋天，他們再往後調一個小時至標準時間，1895 年由喬治・哈德森所提出。這是全球遵循的慣例，但有人質疑值不值得這樣做。例如，因為效率不彰、極度不便，臺灣政府於 1980 年決定放棄日光節約時間。日本、南韓和中國也已取消此計畫。美國有許多州不採用日光節約時間，而一些州正準備廢除。

　　日光節約時間於 1916 年在德國實行，做為節省能源並協助民眾於晚間享有更多日光的方法。然而，一些研究指出，因日光節約時間而省下的能源微不足道。原先也希望多出來的一小時日光能減少交通意外，並鼓勵大家夜間外出消費來振興經濟。但這兩者均未發生。

　　此外，很多人難以適應時間調整，尤其是有睡眠障礙的人。工作時疲累意味著生產力降低。不只有人類被日光節約時間影響，許多農民甚至注意到，雞群在時間調整期間下蛋量變少。現今，這個長達 100 年的慣例恐怕是弊大於利。

■ 正確解答 1.(D) 2.(B) 3.(C)

■ 難題解析

1. 由第一段的內容可知，全文著重在表示日光節約時間的存在價值令人存疑，故選 (D)。
   Main Idea

2. 由文章最後一句提到實行日光節約時間的缺點多於優點，可推知作者對這個習俗抱持負面看法，故選 (B)。　*Purpose and Tone*

3. 由第一段第三句可知，1895 應為喬治・哈德森提出日光節約時間的年份，故 (A) 選項有誤；(B) 選項有誤，可由第三段得知日光節約時間讓睡眠障礙患者更痛苦；(D) 選項有誤，1980 年時僅有臺灣廢棄日光節約時間；(C) 選項是本文主旨，答案選 (C)。
   Supporting Details

高階 (Advanced Level)

- -

荷蘭風力發電

　　荷蘭，這個以迷人風車聞名的國家現在是風力發電開發計畫的世界領導者。荷蘭其中一家鐵路公司—荷蘭鐵路，驕傲地聲稱自 2017 年 1 月起，所有的電力火車已經全靠再生能源風力來運作。

火車該如何由風力發電機獲得動力？事實上，這些電力火車是特別設計過的。比起傳統火車，這些獨特的電力火車沒有引擎，透過輸電網，電力由高壓電線傳送。鐵路網一接收到電力，便會將能源儲存在裝載於列車上的電池。這些電力也供應車上的電燈、空調、煞車、電腦系統，而且車內建置的線路可將沒用掉的多餘電力返還至電網，幫鐵路公司節省電費。根據數據顯示，這項系統每年用上 12 億千瓦的電。但若是和阿姆斯特丹每年用上 15 億千瓦的電相比，我們就會發現風力發電是有開發潛力的。

　　也許你會想知道在這項重大突破之後，下一步是什麼？由於風力發電的潛力振奮人心，荷蘭正打算在北海的人造島上建造廣大的風力發電廠。這個新型的風力發電廠將會取代舊型，並藉著大規模的電力製造降低能源花費。這個發電廠將會供應能源給荷蘭、英國，未來更會供應丹麥、比利時及德國。在未來，我們也許不僅在運輸業，還有其他生活面向都能享受到風力發電的成果。

■ 正確解答 1.(B) 2.(C) 3.(C) 4.(C) 5.(D)

■ 難題解析

1. 文章通篇介紹風力發電為荷蘭所帶來的正面影響，答案選 (B)。　*Main Idea*

3. 由文章中第三段提到荷蘭打算建新型的風力發電廠，可推知該字應有「取代」之意，故選 (C)。　*Words in Context*

4. 第二段解釋火車獲得動力的流程，高壓電線傳送電力至輸電網，鐵路網獲得電力並儲存於電池中，再供應給列車及車上設施，接著再將沒有用到的電傳給輸電網，答案選 (C)。
　Supporting Details

5. 第三段的倒數第二句可知，未來新型風力發電廠所產生的電力，會提供給其他國家，答案選 (D)。　*Supporting Details*

News 時事

初階 (Basic Level)

臺灣瘋夾娃娃

今日新聞

夾娃娃機在臺灣已經開始流行。

今日，臺灣有逾六千家夾娃娃機店。你是否曾經好奇，為什麼最近夾娃娃機店的數量大增？

大家喜歡夾娃娃機似乎是因為很有樂趣。 如果走運的話，一個人只要花新臺幣 10 元就能贏得很酷的獎品。然而，這種情況不常發生。玩家想贏，通常要花較多的錢，而且常常一無所獲。儘管如此，遊戲的刺激感讓他們一玩再玩。對臺主來說，夾娃娃機是很棒的商機。大約新臺幣五千元就能租到一臺夾娃娃機。有人上門玩輸了，臺主就能賺錢。在這樁「懶人生意」裡，臺主唯一要做的事是去添加新獎品和調整夾娃娃的難易度。臺灣有些頂尖夾娃娃機每月能賺進高達新臺幣 15 萬元。

沒人知道夾娃娃機的人氣能持續多久。目前為止，它們似乎仍牢牢抓住了人們的皮夾。

■ 正確解答 1.(C) 2.(A)

■ 難題解析

1. 本篇文章介紹娃娃機在臺灣的瘋狂現象，答案選 (C)。　　*Main Idea*

2. 由前一句可推知，代名詞 they 在此指的是夾娃娃遊戲，答案選 (A)。　　*References*

中階 (Intermediate Level)

趕流行

　　一家電信業者最近以每月新臺幣 499 元的價格推出 4G 不限速吃到飽方案。突然之間，行動通訊門市擠滿了想綁約的消費者。另一波瘋潮發生在日用品商店，因為傳言衛生紙要漲價，大家全湧進店裡搶購囤貨。這些事聽起來很熟悉嗎？你是否也參與其中呢？

　　事實上，這些現象其實是「從眾效應」的例子。這是一個心理學的詞彙，描述追隨他人的行為。在 2008 年，普林斯頓大學的馬修・沙加尼克和鄧肯・華茲進行了一個實驗。他們騙參與者相信，有首歌的人氣高於事實。結果，以為這是暢銷曲的想法，促使參與者未多加考慮就付費下載了這首歌。

　　趕流行的例子無處不在。如果不多加注意，很容易就會被大多數人影響，從在哪裡用餐、該注目什麼、甚至到你應該選擇什麼樣的工作。一旦潮流湧動，就很難停下來！然而，大多數人的決定並不總是正確無誤。在從眾之前，我們真的必須考慮什麼才是最好的。

■ 正確解答 1.(D) 2.(D) 3.(C)

■ 難題解析

1. 由第二段第一句可知，第一段所描述的現象是為了提供例子，讓讀者理解何謂從眾效應，答案選 (D)。　*Main Idea*

2. 由第二段第二句可知，從眾效應一詞是心理學的專有名詞，答案選 (D)。
   Supporting Details

3. 由最後一段倒數第一、二句可知，作者提到占多數的意見並非總是對的，自己仍需花時間思考何者對自身有益，故選 (C)。　*Making Inferences*

高階 (Advanced Level)

臺灣與性別平等

　　因許多權益運動家主張，男人和女人應該得到平等對待，性別平等議題近年來獲得高度矚目。臺灣，這個以民主和自由而聞名的國家，在這個領域已邁開大步前行，且能驕傲地宣稱擁有許多女性領袖，甚至一位女總統。有了這麼大的進步，許多人認為臺灣不再苦於性別不平等問題。你同意這個說法嗎？那麼，看看一些統計數據可能會幫你更了解這個狀況。

　　根據 2016 年主計總處統計，臺灣性別平等的情形在世界排名第 38 名。在政治圈，臺灣的立法委員僅 38% 是女性。在企業界，臺灣企業執行長僅 6% 是女性。至於教育圈的狀況，高中校長和大學校長分別僅有 **25%** 和 **7%** 是女性。可見臺灣婦女仍努力爭取在公領域的能見度。

　　此外，在臺灣，女孩和婦女的生活往往非常艱辛。女孩傾向被教導要有愛心、要溫柔，和做為助力。家庭聚會中，你會發現女性承擔所有家務，而男人只是悠閒坐著。在工作場合，女性經常被要求要化妝和穿著不舒服的商務套裝。

　　雖然臺灣要成為性別平等的國家還有一段很長的路要走，但它並不孤單。身為亞洲自由民主聯盟 (CALD) 的一員，臺灣已從其他會員國得到許多支持，一路上也被授與權力。舉例來說，臺灣已立法為職業婦女創造一個性別友善的環境。也就是超過百名員工的公司，都必須提供育嬰和哺乳的設施。因此，臺灣在性別平等方面確實取得很大進展，我們應該因此感到自豪。

■ 正確解答 1.(B) 2.(B) 3.(B) 4.(C) 5.(A)

■ 難題解析

1. 本文在探討臺灣性別平等議題的狀況，答案選 (B)。　*Main Idea*

2. 第二段的數據是在回應第一段臺灣社會已進步到性別平等的假設。這些數據顯示，仍有努力的空間，答案選 (B)。　*Making Inferences*

3. 這裡的 it 是代替前面已出現過的主詞 Taiwan，答案選 (B)。　*References*

4. 由第三段倒數第二句可知，在家族聚會時，女性時常被要求處理所有家務，而男性才是坐著放鬆的，選項 (C) 有誤，故選 (C)。　*Supporting Details*

5. 從最後一段的最後一句，作者提到臺灣在性別平等上已有長足的進步，且我們應感到驕傲，可推測作者對臺灣性別平等的狀況是正面樂觀的，故選 (A)。　*Purpose and Tone*

初階 (Basic Level)

大型淨灘活動

我們去淨灘

你的穿著與裝備

帽子

領巾

T恤

運動鞋

我們會提供

筆

麻布袋

後背包

水壺

籌辦者：衛斯菲爾德海灘協會
共同籌辦者：海洋淨灘聯盟
贊助者：查理貝果咖啡廳

衛斯菲爾德海灘協會將在 6 月 8 日舉辦淨灘活動。我們希望這會是歷來最大的淨灘活動，所以請帶上幾位朋友或家人——年齡不拘！

今年，查理貝果咖啡店會贊助這次的淨灘活動，將供應每位參加者咖啡和貝果，替他們補充能量並提高工作效率。別忘了帶你自己的環保杯盤來。

我們也會舉辦淨灘比賽。四人一組，比賽看誰能收集到最多垃圾。贏家能獲得神秘獎品！稍後見！

■ 正確解答 1.(A) 2.(D)

■ 難題解析

1. 本文主旨在邀請一般民眾來參加淨灘活動，故選 (A)。　*Main Idea*

2. 由圖片可得知，廠商會提供麻布袋，參加民眾不用自備，故選 (D)。　*Supporting Details*

中階 (Intermediate Level)

綠色遊戲，綠色地球

人類的活動正將大自然推向極限，對環境造成衝擊、改變氣候、並對生物多樣性產生威脅。融化的冰川、森林縮減和沙漠擴大都是大自然的反撲。這些景象提高了環保意識，但是，年輕人要怎樣才能了解環境議題，並採取行動防止情況變得更糟呢？<u>一些新的遊戲和應用程式透過謎題、測驗和虛擬情境教導年輕世代此事的重要性，並展示如何幫助地球。</u>

一款名為「地球入門學」的應用程式是為了愛玩耍的人製作的科學課本。玩家在遊戲開始時可以造山、植林了解地球的運作。然後試著透過指尖創造自然的力量。玩家可以製作火山、雕塑高山、打造冰河、形塑沙丘、移動板塊、彩繪風、加熱岩漿，甚至更多！此外，這款遊戲有即時衛星圖像。如此一來，當天然災害發生，應用程式會告訴玩家那些自然災害是怎麼產生的，並讓玩家互動體驗。透過展示實際發生在地球上的變化，激發玩家對地球更多的關心。

如果年輕人不認識大自然，就不會欣賞和保護它。有越來越多遊戲或應用程式開發出來是為了鼓吹環境保護，希望地球有一天會再變綠。

■ 正確解答 1.(A) 2.(B) 3.(C)

■ 難題解析

1. 整篇文章在說明，一些新遊戲和應用程式透過各種方式傳達環境保護的重要性，答案選 (A)。　*Main Idea*

2. 由文章中的第二段，可知「地球入門學」透過各種互動操作，讓玩家了解環境議題的重要，進而關懷地球，答案選 (B)。　*Supporting Details*

3. 由最後一段可知，這些綠色遊戲是為了提升年輕人對於環境保護的意識，答案選 (C)。　*Supporting Details*

該從我們的塑膠夢魘中醒來了

我們在日常生活中能看到多少塑膠製品？我們已經丟掉了多少？塑膠在我們用完後到哪裡去了？實際上，所有曾經生產出來的塑膠製品一塑膠袋、電腦鍵盤、吸管等等一都仍然存在。塑膠與紙張、織物，甚至是金屬都不一樣，它不容易分解。據說塑膠水瓶要 450 年才能腐爛分解，較厚的塑膠製品會花上兩倍長的時間！

塑膠幾乎堅不可摧，大部分流落入海。一旦到了那裡，會被強大洋流帶到巨大漩渦狀垃圾堆裡。其中最大的被稱為太平洋垃圾帶。這個垃圾帶看起來很嚇人，且對海洋動物產生可怕的影響。例如，每年都有數千隻海龜被塑膠廢棄物纏住不能脫身而淹死，甚至有數量更多的信天翁受到影響。這些大型海鳥以為小塊塑膠是食物，經常將之吞下肚。由於信天翁無法消化塑膠，它會留在牠們的胃裡，使牠們誤以為自己已經吃飽了。結果，這些雄偉的生物每年都要死掉數十萬隻。

我們對這些悲劇負有責任，必須對其採取行動。回收很重要，但這樣還不夠。由於塑膠能存在很長的時間，唯一的解決方案是停止使用。停止使用塑膠袋、停止用多層塑膠包裹食材，並在能選擇可重複使用的替代品時，停止購買拋棄式塑膠製品。我們創造出這個塑膠惡夢，唯有我們才能終結它。

■ 正確解答 1.(A) 2.(C) 3.(C) 4.(D) 5.(D)

■ 難題解析

1. 第一段末提到塑膠不易分解的特性，而這正也是生態噩夢的來源，故選 (A)。

   Supporting Details

2. 文章末段提到停止使用塑膠是唯一的辦法，故選 (C)。　*Supporting Details*

3. 由第二段的上下文推測，此處的代名詞 it 代表塑膠廢棄物，故選 (C)。　*References*

4. 文章第二段提到海洋、海龜和信天翁都是塑膠廢棄物的受害者，而且從最後一段可推測，人類若是袖手旁觀，也會受害，故選 (D)。　*Supporting Details*

5. 本文藉由提問、數據以及生態浩劫的呈現來喚起人們的環保意識，故選 (D)。

   Purpose and Tone

湖南蛋

<u>這是一道叫「湖南蛋」的佳餚，能讓你的餐點更美味。</u>食譜來自中國湖南地區，做起來很簡單。

湖 南 蛋

烹調時間：**25** 分鐘

份數：**2** 至 **3** 人份

烹調難度：簡單

食材配料：

- 4 顆雞蛋
- 3 瓣大蒜
- 1 大匙的麵粉
- 一些剁碎的蔥花和辣椒
- 1 吋新鮮生薑
- 1/2 大匙的醬油
- 3 大匙的橄欖油

作法：

1. 蛋煮 10 分鐘。
2. 蛋殼剝掉，依你個人喜好沙拉呈現的方式切成薄片。
3. 蛋裹粉。
4. 將大蒜和薑切碎。
5. 倒橄欖油入煎鍋，開中火。加入蛋煎 4 分鐘。
6. 加入蒜、醬油、薑、蔥和辣椒，多炒 3 分鐘。持續攪拌混合配料。
7. 將蛋移出煎鍋上菜。

■ 正確解答 1.(A) 2.(A)

■ 難題解析

1. 由文章中的食譜材料可知，購物清單上缺少大蒜，故選 (A)。 *Graphs and Charts*

2. 由文章中的食譜可知，4 個蛋可做出 2 至 3 人份的湖南蛋，Jamie 和朋友共 6 人，大概至少需要 8 個蛋，答案選 (A)。 *Making Inferences*

中階 (Intermediate Level)

小東西大樂趣：扭蛋

數十年來，扭蛋一直風靡日本年輕人。扭蛋是裝在透明塑膠容器裡、從自動販賣機裡掉出來的小玩具，這些玩具有各式各樣的組合，如漫畫角色以及可愛的 LINE 人物。想得到屬於你的扭蛋，你所要做的就是先選一臺販售你喜愛組合的機器、將硬幣投入投幣口、轉動旋鈕，然後等著扭蛋掉出來！

扭蛋於 1965 年首次在日本出現。憑藉低價和吸引人的設計，它很快吸引小孩子的目光。扭蛋玩具非常適合把玩、分享、交易或蒐集。為了展示收藏品，學生把它們掛在書包上，或者擺在書桌上當擺飾。扭蛋可說是每個人童年回憶的一部分。不僅是小孩子，扭蛋玩具更受到各個年齡層的喜愛。

現在扭蛋玩具的品質更好也更精緻，但可能也比以前更昂貴。哪裡可以找到扭蛋？除了便利商店裡普通的扭蛋機以外，顧客還能在東京的電器行和新奇小店裡，找到有出色玩具的名產版扭蛋機。

這些驚奇的扭蛋玩具讓人們的生活增添色彩。你渴求擁有自己的扭蛋嗎？現在就選一個吧！

■ 正確解答 1.(C) 2.(D) 3.(D)

■ 難題解析

1. 文章第二段提及 ，當時扭蛋推出後馬上受到孩童歡迎 ，是因為價格低廉以及設計吸引人，故選 (C)。 *Supporting Details*

2. 文章第三段提到可得到扭蛋的地方並未包括農夫市場，故選 (D)。 *Supporting Details*

3. 文章第二段提到人們可蒐集、交換、買賣以及玩扭蛋玩具，故選 (D)。

Supporting Details

高階 (Advanced Level)

齋戒月：伊斯蘭的聖月

你聽說過齋戒月嗎？**這是在伊斯蘭教的世界中，最重要的日子之一。**穆斯林在伊斯蘭曆的第九個月開始神聖的齋戒月。穆斯林家庭會張燈結綵，打造過節氣氛。穆斯林也在整個齋戒月參加晚禱，唸《古蘭經》，思考信仰在他們生活裡的角色。

齋戒月期間，穆斯林必須從日出齋戒至日落。他們應該要禁絕進食和飲水。齋戒月是為了紀念伊斯蘭教奇蹟：真主阿拉向先知穆罕默德揭示《古蘭經》。因此，穆斯林在這神聖的月分追求精神上的重生。然而，齋戒不僅只是避免飲食，也包括避免惡習，像是說人閒話、抱怨和抽菸。齋戒的目的，是避免因為不好的社會習慣傷害到別人。並且也鼓勵反躬自省和做善事。齋戒月是為了成為一個更好的人以及增進人際關係的時刻。

「開齋節」即表示齋戒月結束。從祈禱開始，簡短的布道，然後是慈善捐贈，穆斯林在開齋節會有三天歡樂假期。為了慶祝，他們穿新衣、給小孩發紅包和零食、造訪親友和掃墓。簡言之，這是個慶祝穆斯林完成一個月禁食的時候。

■ 正確解答 1.(A) 2.(B) 3.(C) 4.(C) 5.(D)

■ 難題解析

1. 本篇文章主要介紹伊斯蘭文化的齋戒月，答案選 (A)。　　*Main Idea*

2. 由第一段的第三句可知，齋戒月的時間在伊斯蘭曆的第九個月，答案選 (B)。

　 Supporting Details

3. 第二段舉出各種禁食、齋戒的例子，最後一句點出齋戒月的意義，答案選 (C)。

　 Making Inferences

4. 由最後一段可知，開齋節為表示齋戒月結束的假日，答案選 (C)。　　*Supporting Details*

History 歷史

初階 (Basic Level)

高雄大樂趣

壽山動物園

六合夜市

愛河

舊打狗驛故事館

複合式按摩咖啡館

駁二藝術特區

　　當你去高雄玩時，可以從愛河開始你的旅程。這是個浪漫且最適合帶約會對象來的地方。遊愛河的最佳方式是搭船。坐在船上，你可以飽覽美麗風景，感受到徐徐微風。此外，到了高雄一定要造訪駁二藝術特區，這個城市最色彩繽紛的其中一個地方。你能欣賞在地藝術家的裝置藝術和壁畫，並看看才華洋溢的街頭藝人，像是雜耍和活雕像的表演者。喜歡動物的人應該花一些時間參觀壽山動物園，只要付合理的入園費，你就能看到臺灣黑熊、白犀牛和其他野生生物。找美食的話，六合夜市是最佳選擇。你可以在那找到許多美味小吃，也可以在那兒買點東西。等你累了，到複合式按摩咖啡館去。你可以邊喝咖啡邊享受按摩，這是個多棒結束此行的方式啊！

■ 正確解答 1.(C) 2.(A)

■ 難題解析

1. 文章中的第五句及第六句，提到駁二藝術特區有許多藝術創作及街頭藝人，答案選 (C)。
   Supporting Details

2. 文章並未提到如何從臺北前往高雄，答案選 (A)。　*Supporting Details*

中階 (Intermediate Level)

馬拉松傳奇

看到 42.195 這個數字，你會想到什麼呢？嗯，長度 42.195 公里是馬拉松比賽的距離。然而，你好奇過人們如何決定馬拉松要跑多長嗎？

大約 2,500 年前，波斯國王想要展示帝國軍力，便派大軍侵略雅典。為了向其他國家求援，雅典人派出了最佳跑者菲迪普斯前往斯巴達。 菲迪普斯兩天內自雅典到斯巴達共跑了大約 240 公里。然而，斯巴達人未如預期地伸出援手。由於敵人快速逼近，菲迪普斯不能浪費時間休息，因此，他又跑了回去。

雖然其他國家幾未馳援，雅典勇敢抗敵，最終贏得戰爭。戰場就在馬拉松，距離雅典約 40 公里遠的城鎮。菲迪普斯知道他的同胞急欲知曉戰事情況，於是飛奔傳達好消息。戰前費力跑了幾百公里、後來又上場打仗，這對他的身體造成了不小的傷害。但菲迪普斯決心不讓國人失望。他雖然疲倦，卻不斷向前跑。

最終，他步履蹣跚地跨進城門，才倒了下來。在嚥下最後一口氣前，他高喊：「好消息，我們打贏了！」雅典人很開心，但同時也為他的過世感到分外難過。之後，馬拉松賽納入現代奧運，而且正是菲迪普斯所跑過的距離。這不僅只是一場比賽，也是向這位為同胞犧牲性命的偉大跑者致敬。

■ 正確解答 1.(D) 2.(B) 3.(D)

■ 難題解析

1. 本文旨在探討馬拉松比賽的由來，答案選 (D)。　*Main Idea*

2. 由第二段第二句可知，菲迪普斯是雅典的最佳跑者，答案選 (B)。　*Supporting Details*

3. 由最後一段可知 ， 奧運馬拉松的距離是為了紀念菲迪普斯當時跑的距離而定 ， 答案選 (D)。　*Supporting Details*

高階 (Advanced Level)

臺灣原住民的正名運動

臺灣原住民逐漸開始盛行使用本名。如《臺北時報》所報導，這項運動有島上名人加持，例如紀錄片導演馬躍・比吼。

1995 年之前，法律規定原住民在官方文件上必須選用中文姓氏及名字，直到 1995 年才修法。從那時起，原住民如果想要的話，可以回復他們原本的原住民姓名。

然而，由於各種不同的理由，許多原住民並未改名。首先，改名可能很麻煩。要改名的話，他們必須到當地戶政事務所處理繁雜的文書資料。大部分的人不願意花時間處理。此外，這僅是過程的第一步。接著，所有其他的正式文件及合約都必須更改。這可能意味護照、電信合約，以及需要中文身分證證明身分的其他許多協定。

除了複雜的行政作業之外，部分原住民擔心要面對來自非原住民的歧視。然而，原住民名字是有其文化意義的。這些名字會是連結族人與歷史的橋樑。有些人甚至相信，這可以讓族人更親近部落文化。

目前，約有 50 萬原住民住在本島。在這些人當中，僅有大約 2 萬人已經選擇回復他們的部落名字。如果改名行動更加盛行，人數在未來可能大幅增加。

■ 正確解答 1.(B) 2.(A) 3.(A) 4.(B) 5.(D)

■ 難題解析

1. 本文第一段提到馬躍・比吼支持原住民正名政策，答案選 (B)。 *Supporting Details*

2. 文章中的第三段提到正名的步驟，並未提到需要將結果登在《臺北時報》上，答案選 (A)。 *Supporting Details*

3. 由第二段的敘述可知，it 在此處指的是採用中文姓氏的法律，答案選 (A)。 *References*

4. 由文章中的第二段，1995 年是正名的分水嶺，答案選 (B)。 *Supporting Details*

5. 文章中提到兩個正名的阻礙：繁瑣的文件程序和受到更多歧視的隱憂，答案選 (D)。 *Supporting Details*

Unit 9

Sport 運動

難忘的籃球賽

　　這是 SSPN 陶德‧洛克的報導。各位先生女生，坐穩了。<u>今晚紐約騎士隊出戰洛杉磯跑者隊，是本年度最精采賽事之一。</u>騎士隊進展很快，你不能錯過明星大前鋒卡爾‧瓊斯。他在第三節得到 20 分。然而跑者隊也沒有放棄。唐尼‧李在第四節火力全開。比賽剩 7 秒鐘時他投進三分球拉平比數。騎士中鋒奧利‧甘耶塔在最後一波進攻時找到空隙，比賽結束前灌籃得分。太不可思議了！我們以前從沒看過甘耶塔這樣打球。以下是數據總結。

比賽日期：2018 年 9 月 22 日　東岸時間晚間 8 點

最高得分者：

| 紐約騎士隊一卡爾‧瓊斯一37 分 | 洛杉磯跑者隊一唐尼‧李一45 分 |

	1	2	3	4	T
NYK	27	23	34	35	119
LAR	31	23	24	39	117

先發陣容

紐約騎士隊		洛杉磯跑者隊
奧利‧甘耶塔	中鋒	瓦帝姆‧普亭
卡爾‧瓊斯	大前鋒	魯本‧馬克斯
朗‧巴克斯	小前鋒	艾瑞克‧亞札利亞
保羅‧尤勒	控球後衛	柯比‧申諾比
達倫‧帕索	得分後衛	唐尼‧李

■ 正確解答 1.(D) 2.(A)

■ 難題解析

1. 根據文章最後的資訊，奧利・甘耶塔在比賽結束前灌籃得分，故選 (D)。

   Supporting Details

2. 根據文章下面列出的數據統計，洛杉磯跑者隊最高得分者唐尼・李得 45 分，而紐約騎士隊的最高得分者卡爾・瓊斯得 37 分，故選 (A)。　*Graphs and Charts*

中階 (Intermediate Level)

電競明星的真實生活

南韓是亞洲運動大國之一。南韓的棒球和足球隊長久以來在世界名列前茅。<u>此外，談到電競 (又稱為電子競技或者電玩)，大家絕不會漏掉南韓。</u>

南韓有數百萬人固定在玩電競。這個國家也有職業電競聯盟和一系列高額獎金大賽。很多場比賽在大型體育館內舉行，數萬名粉絲會到場支持他們最愛的隊伍。

由於對這些活動的高度熱忱，一位頂尖電競玩家的生活其實近似其他的體育明星。他們一天通常花 12 個小時練習打遊戲以增進電玩技能。隨著玩家出名後，他們會有贊助商付錢要他們宣傳服飾和高科技產品。他們賺進大把鈔票的情況並不少見。然而，電競玩家的生活並不像表面看起來那麼多采多姿。即使這聽起來可能像一份輕鬆簡單的工作，這些玩家其實非常辛苦在受訓。

擅長打電玩還不足以登峰造極。必須要勤奮努力和真正投入心力。對大部分人來說，這種程度的投入太多了，他們打電玩只不過為了取樂而已。那你呢？你認為你有潛力攀上電競世界的頂端嗎？

■ 正確解答 1.(D) 2.(B) 3.(A)

■ 難題解析

1. 本題可從前面提到的數萬名粉絲和後面提到最喜愛隊伍，來推測 rooting for 一詞為 supporting (支持) 之意，故選 (D)。　*Words in Context*

2. 文章最後一段提到多數人並無法像電競選手一樣地投入，他們只想為了樂趣而打電動，故選 (B)。　*Supporting Details*

3. 從文章第二和三段提到，電競選手可以藉由參加比賽贏得大筆獎金並且成名，故選 (A)。

   Supporting Details

高階 (Advanced Level)

臺灣之光：蘇祈麟

2018 年 5 月，世界儀隊錦標賽在 (WDC) 佛羅里達州戴通納海灘舉行。正如《自由時報》所報導，臺灣海軍儀隊成員蘇祈麟勇奪第四名。除此之外，他也贏得創辦人特別獎。他和其他 35 名選手同台競技，展現操槍的精湛技巧。**身為首位參與世界儀隊錦標賽的臺灣軍人，蘇祈麟成為臺灣之光。**

做為軍事訓練的一部分，所有士兵都必須經過行軍操演，學習行進隊形。這種操演一開始是為了一個簡單的理由—指揮官需要一個調動大批兵力的方法。而且，這些士兵經常必須長距離行軍。

行軍上戰場時，不同單位經常在同一地點集合。藉由訓練部隊集團行軍，指揮官能將士兵失聯的風險減至最低。經過數個月的行軍操演後，士兵可以集合接受集體號令。時至今日，行軍操練不僅止於踏步前行，還包括特殊的操槍技巧，能在國定節日表演。

在世界儀隊錦標賽，蘇祈麟進行個人表演時有觀眾歡呼加油。為了展現他的操槍神乎其技，他甚至在部分橋段蒙眼演出。表演結束之際，他高喊：「謝謝，世界儀隊錦標賽！謝謝，美國！我愛你，臺灣！」

■ 正確解答 1.(D) 2.(B) 3.(D) 4.(D) 5.(C)

■ 難題解析

1. 文章通篇介紹臺灣之光—蘇祈麟，故選 (D)。　　*Main Idea*

2. 由第一段的最後一句可知，蘇祈麟為首位參與世界儀隊錦標賽的臺灣軍人，答案選 (B)。　　*Supporting Details*

3. 文章中第二段和第三段在解釋行軍的來由和用意，答案選 (D)。　　*Supporting Details*

4. 由最後一段的第二句可知，蘇祈麟為了展現他的操槍神乎其技，於是蒙眼演出，答案選 (D)。　　*Supporting Details*

5. 選項 (A) 有誤，文中並未提到 WDC 每年都在臺灣舉辦；選項 (B) 有誤，並未要求所有指揮官參加世界儀隊錦標賽；選項 (D) 有誤，臺灣是第一次參賽；只有 (C) 正確，故選 (C)。　　*Supporting Details*

Health Care 醫療

初階 (Basic Level)

海倫的處方籤

海倫已經病了好幾天。她發高燒，今天早上甚至還吐了。因此，<u>海倫預約了門診</u>。醫生寫了這份處方箋給她。

家庭診所

104 臺灣臺北市中山區復興北路 123 號

電話：(02) 2234–1234

看診時間：週一至週六　早上 9 點至晚上 10 點。

日期：07 / 25 / 2018　　病歷號碼：000001　　藥單號碼：B0001

姓名：海倫・康洛伊　　性別／年齡：女性／25 歲　　預約號碼：1234567

服用方式與劑量：[口服] 每餐飯後服用藥品各一錠

服用時間：三天

藥品名稱：

　　　Acetaminophen 一錠 500 mg

　　　Domperidone 一錠 10 mg

　　　IWELL 一錠

預防措施：

　　　服藥期間避免飲酒。

內科醫師：麥可・羅倫斯

■ 正確解答 1.(A) 2.(C)

■ 難題解析

1. 由藥單上的資料可知 Helen 的姓氏應為 Conroy，故 (A) 有誤，答案選 (A)。

   Supporting Details

2. 由藥單上內科醫師的署名，可知 Mike Lawrence 在此診所工作，答案選 (C)。

   Supporting Details

中階 (Intermediate Level)

- -

文明病

儘管我們在科技和醫學上有長足的進步，但現代生活根本不利於健康。有許多人長時間工作且花很多時間通勤。那讓我們只剩下有限的時間和精力來準備健康餐點或鍛鍊身體。此外，智慧型手機讓人上癮的本質，造成人們在晚上該睡覺的時間，保持清醒查看手機。

這些不健康的生活型態正侵蝕我們的健康。研究指出，大部分的人正受嚴重的健康問題所苦，像是糖尿病、心臟病、和憂鬱症。**雖然這些健康問題可能是其他因素造成的，但醫學專家卻主張，我們不健康的生活型態就是主因**。讀到這裡，你可能覺得你的未來相當絕望，但事情不需要淪落到這個地步。你可以依循以下步驟，來對抗這些現代的健康問題，也就是所謂的「文明病」。

首先，健康地吃。盡可能多吃新鮮的蔬菜水果。避免太油膩或過度加工的食物。如果可以，你應該少吃泡麵和預熱食品。第二，規律地運動。嘗試騎自行車、游泳或與朋友一起開心運動。找出你喜歡的運動，規律地從事它！最後，花時間與親友相處，以便照顧自己的心理健康，而且晚上要有充足的睡眠。這些事情也許並不容易，但能讓你活得更健康、更快樂、更長壽。

■ 正確解答 1.(B) 2.(C) 3.(C)

■ 難題解析

1. 本篇文章主要介紹文明病，並提供解決此健康問題的方法，答案選 (B)。　*Main Idea*

2. 文章未提到搬到都市可以改善健康，答案選 (C)。　*Supporting Details*

3. 文章中並未提到窮人是否會有文明病，答案選 (C)。　*Supporting Details*

來自《科學怪人》的警告

《科學怪人》是至今仍和現代相關的經典作品之一，因為它讓我們思索科學與倫理道德的<u>關係</u>。例如，許多人不贊成動物實驗，認為這對那些無助的動物來說，既殘酷又痛苦。雖已有許多醫學突破受惠於動物實驗，我們仍然不該視之為理所當然。問題在於，人類比其他動物偉大多少，那些動物是否具有權利並應受到保護。

另一個可能跨越道德界線的例子是基改食物。現在，許多作物經過基因改造，所以不怕除草劑和殺蟲劑。對於農民，這些作物更易栽種、更快收成。但長期來看，「超級雜草」的副作用是否會造成更多的傷害呢？關於基因工程還有另一個議題必須討論。1996 年，科學家已經能利用成年羊隻的細胞培育複製羊。現今，我們雖未準備好迎接複製人，但基因檢測廣泛進行，即將為人父母者可以篩選掉有基因缺陷的胎兒。雖有助於父母在生產前做好準備，但部分人士認為這可能增加墮胎的情形。

如今，科學和倫理道德相纏導致爭議不休。問題不會變得越來越容易解決，只會更加棘手。

■ 正確解答 1.(D) 2.(A) 3.(C) 4.(D) 5.(C)

■ 難題解析

1. 文章通篇介紹科學發展所衍生的道德爭議，答案選 (D)。　*Main Idea*

2. 文章第二段並未提到基因改造會令食物更加美味，答案選 (A)。

   Supporting Details

3. 由第二段第六句可知，複製羊是取出成年羊隻的「細胞」所培育，答案選 (C)。

   Supporting Details

4. 文章中所提出的道德爭議例子，並無有關生病複製體的墮胎議題，答案選 (D)。

   Supporting Details

5. 由最後一段提到，作者認為科學和倫理道德的爭議只會更加棘手，答案選 (C)。

   Purpose and Tone

Travel 旅遊

初階 (Basic Level)

塔拉的假期

這是塔拉第一次到國外旅遊。訂機票前,她將許多城市列入考慮中。例如,她的夢想是去看艾菲爾鐵塔,在巴黎左岸喝杯咖啡,但是機票太過昂貴。許多朋友建議她到曼谷一遊,但塔拉對沙灘和炎熱天氣一點也不感興趣。**最後,她選擇東京為目的地,因為她喜歡日本料理和日本文化。**塔拉在起飛前一個晚上收拾好行李,隔天一早啟程前往機場。

在機場,地勤人員協助她辦理行李報到,並將登機證交給她。現在,在前往登機門前,她正查看航班資訊。

航空公司	航班編號	目的地	起飛時間	登機門	狀態
黃航空	TG-123	曼谷	8:30 a.m.	D3	延誤
紫航空	JL-428	東京	10:00 a.m.	B4	準時
紅航空	CI-724	巴黎	10:25 a.m.	A7	取消

✈ 紫航空　　　　　經濟艙　　　　　登機門 B4

姓名
塔拉‧史密斯

臺北 → 東京

JL-428　　10:00　　14 JUL

登機時間	區域	座位	登機門
9:30	C	20B	**B4**

東京
14 JUL
座位 20B
臺北
10:00
區域 C
姓名 塔拉‧史密斯
JL-428
登機時間 9:30

■ 正確解答 1.(B) 2.(D)

■ 難題解析

1. 由圖表可知,飛往日本的紫航空登機門為 B4,故選 (B)。　*Graphs and Charts*

2. 文章提到塔拉最後決定去日本的原因是因為她喜愛日本的飲食和文化,故可推測塔拉這趟旅程可能會去東京晴空塔參觀和品嚐日本美食,故選 (D)。　*Making Inferences*

到東京晴空塔玩一天

　　我到東京旅遊時，決定一訪該市最知名的建築之一：東京晴空塔。它的高度達 634 公尺，是到目前為止的全球第一高塔。許多日本電視公司從這裡播送節目，取代了老舊的東京鐵塔。**此外，這也是一個主要的觀光景點，能一覽東京美景。**

　　當我從地面仰望晴空塔，對它的設計留下深刻印象。它看起來像一棵來自未來的高科技大樹。當我走進大廳，我很驚訝那裡面有很多室內的設施。訪客能在晴空塔咖啡店裡喝杯咖啡、在晴空塔商店購買紀念品，或是在晴空塔餐廳享受一頓美味餐點。

　　在我來這裡之前，我花了些時間閱讀導覽手冊，天望迴廊是我最想參觀的。買了票之後，我快速地搭電梯到天望迴廊。當我踏出電梯時，看到東京 360 度的完美視野。我能一眼看到全部的地標，像是歷史悠久的佛寺淺草寺，以及富士山。我也透過玻璃地板看到忙碌的大街，這是個有趣且驚喜的經驗。東京晴空塔絕對是我在日本最喜愛的地方之一。所以，如果你有機會到東京一遊，我強烈建議造訪東京晴空塔。

■ 正確解答 1.(D) 2.(C) 3.(B)

■ 難題解析

2. 由第二段可知，晴空塔內有商店，是可以在裡面購買商品的，選項 (C) 有誤，故選 (C)。
   Supporting Details

3. 文章中最後一段，作者強烈建議造訪東京晴空塔，可知作者對這個景點是滿意的，可推測是正面、愉快的感覺，答案選 (B)。　　*Purpose and Tone*

高階 (Advanced Level)

給小費的建議

　　想像你在國外的高檔餐廳享受了一頓美味晚餐。每件事都很完美，直到服務生將帳單遞給你。突然間，你發現你不知道該不該給小費！

　　給服務費，是將少量的錢留給提供你服務的人，一種表達感謝的常見方式。在臺灣，並沒有給小費的慣例，不過全世界對於給小費的看法略有不同。舉例來說，在法國，餐廳帳單內通常會包含服務費，因此給小費就並非必要。然而，法文中的小費所代表的意思是「去喝一杯」。因此，法國人認為給小費是一種友善的表示，來買酒請工作表現好的服務生喝。

　　在羅馬，你應該要入境隨俗。但當談到給小費，卻有點讓人困惑。小費在義大利並非強制，不過，大家負擔得起的話，往往會留一些小費。至於美國，那裡大概是全世界的小費之都。除了餐館，大家在酒吧、計程車和許多其他地方都會留小費，因為美國的服務生薪水並不高。有些人給小費，是把稅金乘上兩倍；其他人則會留帳單總額的 15–20%。不管怎麼做，確保你留些小費，否則別人會認為你很無禮。

　　這些給小費的建議僅僅只是起點而已。在你造訪異國之前，試著花點時間研究他們的小費文化。如此一來，可讓你旅遊時避免一些尷尬的情況。

■ 正確解答 1.(A) 2.(D) 3.(D) 4.(A) 5.(B)

■ 難題解析

1. 文章通篇介紹各國給小費的文化，可推測應該會在「旅遊」類型的書讀到此篇文章，答案選 (A)。　*Making Inferences*

2. 由第二段的第二句提到，全世界各個國家對於小費的看法略有不同，故所提的例子都是為了證明這個論點，答案選 (D)。　*Making Inferences*

4. 由文章中的最後一段可知，在造訪其他國家之前，最好先研究一下該國的小費文化，答案選 (A)。　*Supporting Details*

5. 由第二段的最後一句可知，法國人給小費是一種友善的表示，請工作表現好的服務生一杯酒，選項 (B) 有誤，故選 (B)。　*Supporting Details*

Art 藝術

初階 (Basic Level)

來欣賞穿越歷史的舞蹈

舞蹈年代

日期：2018 年 9 月 22 日星期六

時間：13:30 至 17:00 於威爾森廳

你喜愛跳舞嗎？如果是的話，《舞蹈年代》是屬於你的超棒表演。**這齣音樂劇將呈現舞蹈的歷史。** 此外，你會學到全球各地的流行舞步。感興趣嗎？快來看看節目單吧！

表演時間	年代	節目名稱和舞蹈風格	起源國家
13:30–13:40		開場介紹	
13:40–14:20	中世紀	表達生命歡愉——歐洲舞蹈	歐洲
14:20–15:00	15 世紀末期	英國民俗文化——莫里斯之舞	英國
15:00–15:20		中場休息	
15:20–16:20	1940 年代末期	與諸神對話——曼波	古巴
16:20–16:50	1960 年代中期到 1970 年代初期	夜總會復古風——迪斯可	美國
16:50–17:00		閉幕	

票價資訊

1. 每人新臺幣 1,500 元。(線上訂購可獲 10% 的額外優惠！)

2. 65 歲 (含) 以上的年長者出示身分證能獲得八折優惠。

3. 有大人陪同的 7 歲及以下幼童可免費入場。

4. 附有面積 50 英畝的免費停車空間。

5. 軍公教人員享有票價七折的特殊優惠。

6. 服務臺備有輪椅或嬰兒推車，以供特殊需求。

■ 正確解答 1.(C) 2.(A)

■ 難題解析

1. 由票價資訊可知，一位七歲以上的小孩及 Nathan 共兩張新臺幣 1,500 元的全票、兩張年長者八折的票、一張 Nathan 妻子軍公教人員的七折票以及一張七歲以下小孩的免費票，1,500 × 2 + 1,500 × 0.8 × 2 + 1,500 × 0.7 = 6,450，答案選 (C)。

   Making Inferences

2. 從節目表上的敘述，英國的「莫里斯之舞」可能 Lucy 會最有興趣，答案選 (A)。

   Making Inferences

中階 (Intermediate Level)

- -

百老匯成為劇院首都

位於曼哈頓市中心的百老匯，許多家知名劇院都位於此處。百老匯在 1800 年代晚期和 1900 年代初期頗為著名，當劇院業主為了尋找比市內其他地區租金更便宜的地方而搬到那裡。如今，百老匯是個有趣且忙碌的地方，有一大堆招牌、人、燈光和活動。有數十家劇院在百老匯，有些很大且聲名遠播，其他一些則相對來說較小而且沒什麼名氣。

最大與最知名的劇院之一是美琪劇院，上演過《鳳宮劫美錄》和《歌劇魅影》等大型音樂劇作品，後者是百老匯歷史上演出最久的戲。能演出這麼知名的戲，使美琪劇院贏得絕佳觀劇地點的響亮名聲。

作為觀眾，你可能會訝異於推出一齣精彩好戲要付出多少努力。舞臺上的表演者絕對是明星，但那些在幕後工作的人，例如化妝師、布景設計師、搭景工人、製片人、導演，以及其他專業人士，都是一齣戲獲致成功不可或缺的一部分。拜這些人所賜，我們才有《芝加哥》、《貓》和《悲慘世界》等暢銷作品，到目前為止總計演出逾 25,000 場。

下次，當你有機會參觀百老匯，不要只當個和景點及招牌拍照的觀光客。買張票坐下來看場表演。那不僅會是一次難忘的經驗，也真正支持了奉獻給劇院的人們。

■ 正確解答 1.(D) 2.(C) 3.(D)

■ 難題解析

1. 本文通篇介紹百老匯的起源及戲劇成功之因，答案選 (D)。　　*Main Idea*

2. 第一段提及許多知名劇院在百老匯，可知是劇迷們朝聖之處，答案選 (C)。

   Supporting Details

3. 由第三段第二句可知，文章中戲劇成功的因素並沒有提到預算，答案選 (D)。

   Supporting Details

禪繞畫

　　禪繞畫是透過描繪有組織的圖案，進而創造出美麗設計的方法。雖然成品可能看起來像我們在課本上的塗鴉，但事實上，禪繞畫涉及一種理論及固定過程。芮克・羅伯茲和瑪莉亞・湯瑪斯最先確立禪繞畫的理論和方法。基本上，這是用針筆在白紙上描繪圖案的方法。<u>時至今日，它在全世界愈發流行，被廣泛應用在教室、臨床心理學、藝術治療和靜坐冥想。</u>

　　雖然要完成整幅禪繞畫似乎很複雜，但它僅是點和線構成。各種年齡層的人都能從書上或網路上掌握禪繞畫。對於冥想的人，禪繞畫藝術創作讓他們覺得放輕鬆並專注心神。此外，專家說禪繞畫具有療癒效果，因為每個人畫禪繞畫時不會有任何期待和壓力，你只需要拿起筆來玩，接受眼前景象，別多想。同時，你也能從過程中學會改造錯誤並修改圖像。這是亡羊補牢的人生技巧。

　　在學會禪繞畫的技巧後，作圖可以越來越隨心所欲。這種活動鼓勵人不要太目標取向、別太好勝。它教大家享受生活的當下。透過享受創造過程，你會開始感激每一瞬間，享受個人的創造力。禪繞畫教人「不要心急。暫停下來欣賞今時此刻。」難怪有越來越多人沉迷於禪繞畫的世界。

■ 正確解答 1.(C) 2.(B) 3.(D) 4.(C) 5.(A)

■ 難題解析

1. 文章第一、二段主要是對禪繞畫作簡單的介紹，從中可以得知是一種利用點和線構圖的特殊作畫方式，故選 (C)。　*Main Idea*

2. 由文章中第二段第二句可知，從書或網路上即可學習禪繞畫，答案選 (B)。
　Supporting Details

3. 文章中提到禪繞畫的特點是透過點和線的構圖，不預先設限也不用擔心畫錯，純粹專注在創作當下的快樂與放鬆，答案選 (D)。　*Supporting Details*

4. 從文章中可知，禪繞畫具有舒壓的功效，推測 Christopher 會受益最多，答案選 (C)。
　Making Inferences

5. 文章最後一段提及禪繞畫給人的幫助，並未提到能更快達成個人目標，選項 (A) 有誤，故選 (A)。　*Supporting Details*

Career 職場

婚禮當日相片

寄件人：蘿倫・史密斯 <lauren.smith@gmail.com>

收件人：時髦攝影 <contact@snappyphotos.com>

附本 ：奧斯卡・黑爾波 <oscar.h2018@gmail.com>；保羅・史密斯 <paulsmith8811@ttcomapny.com>

主旨：婚禮照片

2018 年 7 月 24 日　13:28

親愛的時髦攝影：

　　我已收到我的婚禮相片及影片，然而我並不滿意。許多相片模糊或曝光過度。我覺得攝影師應將他的相機升級或購買新的鏡頭。

　　影片稍微好一點。然而，攝影師並沒有照我們交待的做。我們希望賓客可以對著攝影機說幾句有關這特別日子的感言，但他在十桌只有拍了兩桌。

　　我認為時髦攝影應該設法改善此狀況。我覺得我該獲得道歉和部分退款。也許不是全額退款，但要有一些你們公司願為這些錯誤負起責任的表示。

蘿倫・史密斯　敬啟

■ 正確解答 1.(D) 2.(C)

■ 難題解析

1. 本文章為一封不滿意婚禮攝影的抱怨電子郵件，故選 (D)。　*Main Idea*

2. 從文章最後一段， Lauren 要求 Snappy Photos 要道歉， 並退回一些錢， 可知答案選 (C)。　*Making Inferences*

中階 (Intermediate Level)

男女同工同酬嗎？

　　貝絲和查爾斯是為同一家公司效力的經理。他們有同樣的工作職稱，以及類似的工作資歷。他們大部分的同事同意，他們帶給公司的價值不相上下。然而，貝絲的薪水少了 20%。這是因為職場有性別薪資差距。

　　性別薪資差距是潛藏的慣例，付給男性的薪水高於女性。 雖然許多公司聲稱他們沒有這麼做，但數據顯示並非如此。研究指出，全職工作的女性比男性少賺 20%。部分人士聲稱，這是因為男女選擇不同的職業。然而，性別薪資差距在同一個行業中仍然存在。例如，在美國，超過 **70%** 的教師是女性，但是男教師的平均薪資卻高約 13%。同樣的事也發生在業務員、律師和其他好幾個領域。

　　2009 年，當時的美國總統歐巴馬簽署了《莉莉・萊德貝特公平薪酬法》。然而，許多女性仍覺得改變還不夠快。女性的薪資目前仍然比男性低。事實上，以現在進步的速度，部分專家宣稱，同工同酬可能要等上 98 年。但願社會能夠找到一些方法終止性別歧視，支付女性應得的酬勞。

■ 正確解答 1.(D) 2.(B) 3.(D)

■ 難題解析

1. 文章第一段以例子說明性別薪資差距，第二段更進一步用數據解釋男女同工不同酬的現象，故選 (D)。　*Main Idea*

2. 從最後一段，代名詞 it 的前後文可知，it 所代表的是同工同酬這項議題，答案選 (B)。
   References

3. 文章第二段提到性別薪資差距存在於各個職業中，故 (A) 有誤；文章第二段提到雖然美國有超過 70% 的教師是女性，但男性教師的薪水還是高於女性教師，故 (B) 有誤；最後一段提到，專家預測要達到性別間同工同酬可能需要 98 年之久，故 (C) 有誤；文章最後提到希望能解決性別歧視問題，以達到同工同酬的目的，故選 (D)。　*Supporting Details*

掌握職人精神

東京一家小壽司店的吧臺後方，一位主廚正在工作。他小心翼翼地把每片生魚片放到醋飯上捏成形。雖然他捏壽司已經超過 50 年，但他相信自己仍有進步空間。這就是「職人」精神。

「職人」的概念是日本文化中很重要的一部分。雖然職人經常被定義為大師級工匠，但這個詞彙字面的解釋無法精確表達其深層意義。除了高超技巧外，職人的職責還必須深刻關懷社會，以及他們服務的人群。**雖然不可能達到完美境界，但職人應該維持專注，日復一日精益求精。**

不管你選擇了哪一行，成為職人的原則都能幫你保持正向、工作更有效率。這裡提供幾個訣竅可牢記於心。嘗試以整潔乾淨的工作環境開始新的一天。井然有序的工作空間可以讓你專注並提升你的創造力。其次，培養正面的態度，認真看待工作，即使它很無聊。如果你一直重覆一項簡單任務，試著完全專注。一整天都試著思考，能改進例行任務的狀況。時日一久，這些小小的進步能累積下來，大大提升你的工作品質。同時，不要害怕有一點擇善固執。雖然職人應該傾聽別人的意見，但最要緊的就是信任自己的眼光。

最後，也是最該牢記的職人精神特質是熱情。為了達到最高層次的成功，你必須熱愛你在做的事。在職人世界裡，不全力以赴，就不可能成就偉大藝術。

■ **正確解答** 1.(C) 2.(B) 3.(D) 4.(A) 5.(C)

■ **難題解析**

1. 文章第二段的第一句提到，職人的概念是日本文化中很重要的一部分，故選 (C)。
   Supporting Details

2. 從文章第一段可知，職人相信自己仍有進步空間；從文章的第三段可知，專注可以造就優質的品質；而文章的第四段則提到對自己的工作有熱情非常重要，只有選項 (B) 未被提及，故選 (B)。　*Supporting Details*

3. 文中雖提到重複同一個簡單的動作，但也正是不怕麻煩才成就職人，答案選 (D)。
   Supporting Details

4. 本篇文章主要介紹「職人精神」，適合放在生涯探討的指南中，故選 (A)。
   Making Inferences

5. 文中提到職人精神的重點：不斷求進步、服務人群社會、以及熱情，選項 (C) 與職人精神無關，故選 (C)。　*Making Inferences*

Disaster Prevention 防災

---

816 島發生地震

上週五早上 **8** 時過後不久，**816** 島發生一場嚴重的地震。下午又有一個熱帶風暴襲擊該島，令情況雪上加霜。暴風雨帶來時速 **75** 英里的強風，且在 **10** 小時內降雨量達 **20** 公釐。稍早報導指出，許多人因此而受傷甚至死亡。此外，數千人無家可歸。專家相信，這場災難造成的損失超過 **130** 億元。有好幾個國家已經提供支援。例如，美國和法國已經派遣醫療團隊、送來日用品，以及近一千萬美元的人道救援。

地震資訊

地點：816 島

時間日期：2018/8/16 上午 8:03

地震強度：6.4

受傷人數：324 人

死亡人數：53 人

無家可歸：7,000 人 (預估)

經濟損失：130 億元 (預估)

捐獻：1,000 萬元 (截至目前為止)

■ 正確解答 1.(C) 2.(A)

■ 難題解析

1. 由文章中的第四句與圖表可知，根據報導，災難中的受傷人數為 324 人，答案選 (C)。
   Supporting Details

2. 由文章中最後一句可知，其他國家並未提供社區復原，答案選 (A)。　　*Supporting Details*

中階 (Intermediate Level)

臺灣核電引發關注

　　2011 年，日本的一場天災給全球都帶來震撼。大地震以及隨之而來的核能危機不僅在日本造成問題，也引發其他國家的疑慮。**處於地震斷層帶上的臺灣，需借鏡日本並重新思考核電的未來**。

　　臺灣沒有礦物燃料蘊藏，選擇了核能發電已數十年。目前有三座現役核電廠、六座反應爐，全由臺灣電力公司 (臺電) 負責管理。根據統計數據，核能發電占臺灣全國能源消耗的近 10%。現在，日本福島第一核電廠的危機讓許多人懷疑臺灣核電廠的安全性。

　　一些報導顯示，位於新北市萬里的國聖核電廠也許存在不安全狀況。更具體的說，該電廠抑壓池據說有大量沉積物、殘礫和廢棄物，遇緊急狀況可能非常危險。一位臺電發言人卻表示，這些地方都清理過，國聖廠也安排了定期清除作業。而且，還有人指出，臺灣核電廠使用的沸水式反應爐，和日本福島第一核電廠的反應爐類似。

　　反核人士在日本核災之後聚集凱達格蘭大道抗議。他們向政府訴求「反核，不要再有下一個福島」。政府在能源需求和環境之間該如何拿捏平衡點，會是一大挑戰。

■ 正確解答 1.(B) 2.(C) 3.(B)

■ 難題解析

1. 由第二段第二句可知，臺灣目前正運作的核電廠共有三座，答案選 (B)。
   Supporting Details

2. 由第三段的最後一句可知，人們之所以對核能產生疑慮的其中一個原因，就是反應爐和日本福島核電廠的類似，答案選 (C)。　　*Supporting Details*

3. 由最後一段提到，要拿捏能源和環境之間的平衡點，可推論若此篇文章仍有續集，應會討論核能的替代方案，答案選 (B)。　　*Making Inferences*

高階 (Advanced Level)

- -

防災準備

　　地震、龍捲風、海嘯、火山爆發和颱風——這些天然災害有何共同之處？它們都難以預測但又無可避免。這就是為什麼人們面對天然災害會擔心害怕。在臺灣，地震和颱風是兩大威脅，兩者都威力大到足以摧毀一切。災後的土石流或洪水可能損害房舍和讓人無家可歸。**然而，我們心裡若有認識並做好準備，發生天然災害時，就能更快、更好地因應。**

　　以下是一些可供遵循的指示。說到颱風的話，留在室內會是最好的選擇。確保你在家裡儲有足夠的水和食物。上下檢查周圍區域，確保下大雷雨也不會淹水。此外，由於可能斷電，你必須準備手電筒和備用電池，以防萬一。至於地震，有必要定期舉行地震演習，因為地震發生前沒有預警。確保你知道疏散路線，隨時保持通暢無阻。手邊有逃生包是明智選擇。當搖晃過度到失控時，你可以考慮盡快離開你所在的建築物。

　　天然災害也許無法避免，但藉由事先規劃，我們可以獲得較高的機會生存。如同諺語說「預防勝於治療」，為天然災害預作準備不會有害。

■ 正確解答 1.(C) 2.(B) 3.(B) 4.(A) 5.(B)

■ 難題解析

1. 文章通篇介紹天然災害，並提供方法及步驟教導讀者如何預防，答案選 (C)。
   Main Idea

2. 第一段的第四句提到，臺灣時常面臨的天然災害是地震和颱風，答案選 (B)。
   Supporting Details

3. 由第一段第二句可知，人們害怕天然災害，是因為它們都難以預測但又無法避免，答案選 (B)。　*Supporting Details*

4. 第二段提到針對颱風的預防方式，並未提到迅速離開家中，而是應該留在室內，故 (A) 有誤，答案選 (A)。
   Supporting Details

5. 由文章中最後一段可知，此諺語和「預防」相關，選項 (B) 意為「一天一蘋果，醫生遠離我」同樣有預防的意思，答案選 (B)。　*Words in Context*

20分鐘稱霸統測英文字彙

陳曉菁／編著

- 篩選近年統測常考的單字與近義詞組，補充豐富字詞用法、同義字與通用搭配。
- 20回練習題符合近年統測出題趨勢，取材多元，可培養生活知識素養。
- 解析夾冊加碼「單字隨身GO」單元，背單字、複習帶這本就夠！

統測致勝關鍵：
英文考前18週總複習

王櫻珍、方麗閔　編著

考前18週最後衝刺，贏戰統測這本就夠！
彙整統測重點精華，瞄準統測各種題型，量身打造複習計畫。

字 彙 題：精選統測高頻字彙與課綱議題字彙，補充同反義字與搭配用
　　　　　法，擴充單字力！

對 話 題：歸納統測最常出現的生活情境對話，統整對話中常見實用句
　　　　　型，提升應答力！

綜合測驗：涵蓋多種主題選文，充分演練單字、片語、轉折詞與句型文
　　　　　法，增強解題力！

閱讀測驗：因應命題趨勢，提供「素養閱讀題組」和「長篇閱讀」，培
　　　　　養多元文本閱讀力！

非選擇題：精心編寫統測填充、中譯英、句子重組等非選題型，取材廣
　　　　　泛，強化應試力！

三民東大學習平台
elearning.sanmin.com.tw